GW00371992

704

checked

Dr. Heidi's

ANTI-AGING
COOKBOOK

Creative Recipes for Cooking
with Power Foods

HEIDI REGENASS M.D.

Published by
R&R Publications Marketing Pty Ltd
ABN 78 348 105 138

12 Edward Street, Brunswick
Victoria 3056, Australia
Phone: (61 3) 9381 2199
Fax: (61 3) 9381 2689
E-mail: info@randrpublications.com.au
Website: www.randrpublications.com.au,
www.rrphotostudio.com.au

©Heidi Regenass, 2007

Publisher: Anthony Carroll
Production Manager: Neil Hargreaves
Graphic Designer: Elain Wei Voon Loh
Photographs of Dr. Regenass: Jeff Newton
(www.jeffnewton.com)
Food Photography: Brent Parker Jones,
R&R PhotoStudio
Food Stylist: Lee Blaylock, Sebastian Sedlak
Proofreader: Stephen Jones

The National Library of Australia
Cataloguing-in-Publication Data
Author: Regenass, Heidi

Dr. Heidi's Anti-Aging Cookbook: Creative
Recipes for Cooking with Power Foods

ISBN 978-1-74022-649-3 (hbk)
Subjects: Diet – Nutritional Aspects, Aging
– Prevention, Cookery (Natural Foods), Health
Dewey Number: 641.563
First Edition Printed December 2007

All rights reserved. No part of this book
may be stored, reproduced or transmitted
in any form or by any means without written
permission of the publisher, except in the
case of brief quotations embedded in critical
articles and reviews.

Distributed in Australia by
New Holland Publishers (Australia) Pty Ltd
1/66 Gibbs Street, Chatswood NSW
Phone: (61 2) 9417 1522
Fax: (61 2) 9417 2422

Printed in Singapore

Disclaimer: The information contained in this book is presented for the purpose of educating
people. Every effort has been made to make this book as accurate as possible. Nothing
contained in this book should be construed as, nor is it intended to be used for, medical
diagnosis or treatment. It should not be used in place of the advice of your physician or
other qualified health-care provider. Always consult with your physician or other qualified
health-care provider before starting a new treatment, diet or fitness program.

Any application of the information herein is at the reader's own discretion and risk. Therefore,
any individual with a specific health problem or who is taking medication must first seek
advice from their personal physician or health-care provider before starting a nutrition
program. The author and publishers shall have neither liability nor responsibility to any person
or entity with respect to loss, damage, or injury caused or alleged to be caused directly or
indirectly by the information contained in this book.

The moral right of the author has been asserted.

CONTENTS

Introduction	4
Breakfast	18
Soups	32
Salads	60
Main Courses	82
Vegetable Dishes	118
Side Dishes	142
Desserts	160

introduction

INTRODUCTION

My goal is to share with you my knowledge of healthy, nutrient-dense, antioxidant foods and to provide you with quick and easy ways to prepare delicious healthy dishes utilizing these power foods.

As a child, I had the great fortune of growing up in Zimbabwe in Southern Africa. The soil was fertile and farming was a mainstay of the economy. Local farms dotted the beautiful countryside and surrounded the city neighborhoods. We had the luxury of purchasing daily farm-fresh meats, poultry and organic fruits and vegetables, from which we would then prepare delicious, healthy meals.

From an early age I learned to cook at the apron strings of Winnie, our family cook and "second mother". I enjoyed planning the daily meals with Winnie, accompanying her to the market and assisting her in the kitchen. Winnie taught me the importance of using fresh ingredients, and the art of seasoning with just the right herbs and spices. From my time in the kitchen with Winnie, I gained a true appreciation and love for healthy foods and the important role they play in one's health and well-being.

Prior to going to medical school, I earned a Master's Degree in Health Education. With this degree I developed and instructed various health education courses, teaching patients how to follow a nutritious diet and avoid situations that had led or were leading to conditions like diabetes, heart disease, obesity and premature aging. During medical school I had the opportunity to learn more in-depth the effects that proper and improper nutrition have on the body's ability to function. During my surgery training I saw firsthand the body from the inside out and the consequences of one's dietary choices, good and bad. The knowledge I received from my education, training and work experiences instilled in me a desire to share the importance of proper nutrition and how it can affect the aging process. I thought to myself, what better way to do this than through a cookbook? Cooking, to me, is one of my greatest forms of relaxation and is my favorite creative outlet. I enjoy spending hours in the kitchen combining ingredients to create new and healthy dishes. For me, preparing unique, nutritious meals is a passion and a wonderful escape.

My goal is to share with you my knowledge of healthy, nutrient-dense, antioxidant foods and to provide you with quick and easy ways to prepare delicious healthy dishes utilizing these power foods. These recipes will help you to look and feel your best, and slow the aging process from the inside out.

ANTI-AGING

Power Foods – Our Mothers Were Right

It is no secret that proper nutrition plays a key role in maintaining a strong and healthy body. In the last few years there has been a heightened interest in certain foods that are often referred to as power foods or superfoods. These foods have been singled out for their high levels of nutrients, and for their roles in reducing the risk of many diseases and the symptoms of premature aging. Nearly everyone can list one or two power foods, however, the list of these disease-fighting, longevity-promoting foods is quite long. Many of the foods on the list are those that our mothers insisted we finish before leaving the table. Much has been written about these foods and their roles in promoting health and fighting disease. However, one thing that I see often in my line of work is that many people do not connect healthy food choices with appearance and aging.

Aging and Appearance – Simply Speaking

The process and visible signs of aging occur for a variety of reasons. Every day our skin is subjected to the ravages of the environment through exposure to the sun, pollution, cigarette smoke, poor diet and stress, among other things. Exposure to these elements causes the formation of free radicals, which damage the cells in the body. Muscle movement generates another symptom of aging – when we move our facial muscles to communicate, eat and show emotion, muscle contraction can result in expression lines on the face. Stress and anxiety can also affect many of the processes in the body. Stress hormones in the body promote destruction of cells, which increases the risk of disease and the visible signs of aging. All of these factors combine to result in skin/tissue laxity, lines and wrinkles.

The Good News – Diet Can Defy Aging

We can enhance our skin's ability to repair itself, and fortify ourselves against further damage, through the consumption of foods high in antioxidants. Antioxidants are very important because they neutralize free radicals. Free radicals damage collagen and elastin, the support structures of the skin, so that our complexion becomes dull and the skin starts to become loose and wrinkled with uneven pigmentation. We can further protect our skin from aging by using sunscreen and skin-care products containing antioxidants.

As a plastic surgeon, I have the opportunity to see the aging process from the inside out. I have many tools at my disposal to improve the appearance of the skin, from skin-care products to surgery and everything in between. But it is shortsighted to only focus on the outside of the skin. A diet high in nutritious, anti-aging power foods can help to protect the body and heal the skin from the inside out. Both internal and external aspects are required for overall skin health and to slow the aging process.

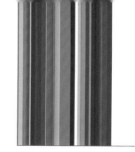

Anti-Aging – From the Inside Out

Anti-aging in general has to do with the body as a whole, not just the skin. In my emphasis on holistic health, I think it is important to look at some other key components of anti-aging and wellness. Certainly, we focus on the skin since we can see the effects of aging so obviously there. But we must also remember that aging happens inside the body as well. This is why diet and proper nutrition are so important. Antioxidants found in fruits and vegetables help to minimize the damage to cells from free radicals. Inflammation is another culprit as it speeds up the aging process – this can affect the heart, brain and blood vessels, contributing to heart disease, dementia, diabetes and elevated cholesterol levels.

WHOLE GRAINS

Contrary to popular belief, carbohydrates are not the enemy. But keep in mind that there are good and bad carbohydrate choices. Fruits, vegetables and whole grains are all healthy carbohydrate choices with anti-aging benefits. Modified carbohydrates such as refined flour and sugar, and foods made from them, are the kinds of carbs to avoid because of their low nutrient and fiber value and their resultant rapid swings in blood sugar. High levels of blood sugar also promote inflammation, which causes cells to age sooner than they should. Our diet must be regulated to avoid such spikes in blood sugar levels.

Whole grains provide that regulation and simultaneously decrease inflammation in the body. They are a vital part of an anti-aging diet, as they naturally regulate blood sugar.

Wheat in its natural and unrefined state is extremely nutritious, because it includes bran and germ, high-fiber components that are removed from refined flours.

Making the switch to whole grains is actually easier than you might think, given the number of options in the supermarket today. Choose wholewheat flour and wholegrain breads, pasta, tortillas and cereals, and brown rice instead of white. Incorporate grains such as quinoa, buckwheat and millet into your diet. These are nutrient-rich, complex carbohydrates that also contain essential amino acids, making them a good source of protein as well. These fiber-rich foods slow digestion, thereby helping to regulate blood sugar levels.

FRUITS AND VEGETABLES

Fruits and vegetables are among the greatest sources of antioxidants because they contain essential phytonutrients – naturally occurring plant compounds that gobble up free radicals.

Individuals who consume a diet rich in fruits and vegetables experience increased energy, less propensity to gain weight, and a decreased risk of disease. When selecting fruits and vegetables, remember that darker colors – deep greens and reds – typically mean higher levels of nutrients. Also, whenever possible, try to select foods that are organically grown, as these are free of pesticides, which can induce cell damage. The higher levels of antioxidants in fruits and vegetables grown organically give you "more bang for your buck". Eat several servings daily.

LEAN PROTEIN

Protein is a key ingredient in cellular renewal and repair, acting as a building block for damaged muscle, skin, cartilage and bones. In modest quantities, quality dietary protein can encourage beautiful skin and healthy tissues.

Incorporate vegetarian, lean meat and fish sources of protein into your diet. Legumes such as garbanzo, kidney, black and white beans, as well as lentils, make delicious fiber-rich, high-protein meals. Lean meats,

including free-range and/or organic chicken and turkey served skinless, are quick and easy to prepare as well. Fish, such as salmon, cod, trout, tuna, and halibut, are also excellent sources of quality protein. Remember to eat wild salmon and trout instead of farm-raised whenever possible.

Nuts such as almonds, pecans, and walnuts can be incorporated into meals and eaten as high-protein, fiber-rich snacks. Add flaxseed meal and wheat germ to baked goods, cereals, and to your favorite smoothie for heart-healthy protein. Also, eggs are fine when eaten in moderation. Choose free-range and omega-3 fatty acid enriched eggs if available.

HEALTHY FATS

Healthy fats are an essential part of a good diet – but the key word is "healthy". Monounsaturated fats, such as extra-virgin olive oil and nut oils, as well as nuts, avocados, and vitamin E, provide powerful antioxidant defenses.

Non-hydrogenated butter and margarine spreads are, in fact, acceptable alternatives. I often use Earth Balance natural buttery spread in my recipes. Avoid partially hydrogenated, trans and saturated fats. Use of such fats can lead to accelerated aging by promoting inflammation and heart disease.

HERBS AND SPICES

Herbs and spices are one of nature's best-kept anti-aging secrets. Many have tremendous health benefits and are excellent sources of antioxidants. Herbs and spices with anti-inflammatory effects are beneficial because they can slow the aging process of cells.

Below are a few examples, along with their health benefits – there are, of course, many others. Incorporating them into your daily meals will provide another source of powerful antioxidants.

Ginger has a strong anti-inflammatory effect, and strengthens the immune system.

Basil helps to protect your DNA, reduces inflammation, and protects your cardiovascular system.

Rosemary helps to stimulate the immune system, improves the circulatory system, and assists in digestion.

Turmeric lowers cholesterol, acts as a strong anti-inflammatory, and may improve liver function.

Black pepper has a great antioxidant effect, and may help with the breakdown of fat cells.

Cinnamon acts as a powerful antioxidant and may aid in controlling blood sugar.

WATER AND TEAS

Hydrate, hydrate, hydrate! And don't ever let yourself get thirsty – drink enough before this ever happens. Water is one of the most important factors in decelerating the aging process. Unlike today's popular carbonated beverages and coffees, water actually hydrates the body, giving what is needed for optimal performance.

Working at a cellular level, water helps rid the body of waste, keeps joints lubricated, lessens the chance of kidney stones, prevents and lessens the severity of colds and flu, and can help prevent constipation. When combined with certain herbs to make tea, water can pack a potent restorative punch, filled with a vital boost of antioxidants.

Green tea, rooibos (red bush) and honeybush teas are widely touted for their antioxidant benefits. My personal favorite is rooibos, a tea native to a unique region in South Africa. I grew up drinking this antioxidant powerhouse tea that is naturally caffeine-free and low in tannins. This particular tea has been used for centuries by local inhabitants of South Africa's Cederberg mountains. It has even higher levels of antioxidants than green tea. In my medical practice, I have even used it as a cooling spray on the faces of my surgical patients for its soothing effects.

VITAMINS AND MINERAL SUPPLEMENTS

Consider supplementing your diet with multivitamins that contain antioxidants. This additional step acts as an insurance policy, augmenting your healthy diet. Make sure that you choose a supplement that will provide you with the recommended daily allowances of essential vitamins and minerals. Remember to always consult with your doctor prior to starting or altering any supplementation regimen.

EXERCISE

Any healthy, anti-aging lifestyle is not complete without exercise, but that doesn't mean you have to live in the gym. The key is to choose an appropriate exercise that you enjoy and that fits your lifestyle and energy levels, and then do it regularly. After-dinner walks, swimming, aerobics, hiking, dancing, rollerblading and gardening are all forms of exercise that can have a lasting impact on your health and vitality.

Regular exercise can have tremendous anti-aging benefits, protecting you from stroke, heart disease, high blood pressure, obesity, and osteoporosis. It can also positively affect your mood by activating the neurotransmitters serotonin and norepinephrine – chemicals used by the nerve cells that regulate mood. Exercise also helps produce endorphins that produce feelings of relaxation and well-being. It's absolutely one of the best ways to de-stress.

To ensure the maximum health benefit, you should complete 20–30 minutes of aerobic activity three or more times a week, in addition to some type of muscle strengthening activity and/or stretching at least twice a week. If free weights are too intimidating, consider using strength training resistance bands, which provide a great alternative. It is important to remember that before starting any exercise program you should consult with your physician.

SLEEP AND REST

Adequate sleep and rest are essential components of good health. During sleep the body repairs itself from daily environmental and internal stresses and the immune system is strengthened. Sleep can also assist in regulating certain chemicals and hormones – such as melatonin and cortisol – necessary for bodily functions. Healthy ranges of cortisol help prevent cell damage. Additionally, it is very important to learn how to relax and give your body the chance to heal from the onslaught of daily stresses. Aim for 7–8 hours of uninterrupted sleep each night. Regular exercise can help you sleep better, but try to avoid exercising less than 4 hours before going to bed.

WELL-BEING

Another component to holistic anti-aging involves social connections and spiritual well-being. Love, relationships and spirituality are key components of longevity. Studies have shown that people with more social support not only have a better quality of life, but can extend their lives as well. Visit with family and friends often. Schedule special time with your significant other. Stimulate your mind as you would your body — make lifelong learning part of your healthy, anti-aging lifestyle. And remember the adage — "use it or lose it".

COOKING WITH POWER FOODS

Awareness regarding anti-aging, health and wellness has grown tremendously in the last few years, and more and more people are realizing that healthy food choices play a vital role in feeling good and looking great. Power foods are now widely recognized for their health benefits and their role in anti-aging medicine.

This book provides a comprehensive list of the key power foods and the health benefits they provide, before showing you how to prepare them in quick and easy recipes. I hope you'll be inspired to make these foods a part of your daily diet, thereby contributing to a healthier, happier, more gorgeous you. Bon appetit!

ANTI-AGING POWER FOODS

ALLIUM
garlic
leeks
onions
scallions
shallots

COCOA
cocoa powder
dark chocolate

FRUITS
açai
apples
apricots
avocados
bananas
blackberries
blueberries
cantaloupe
cranberries
grapefruit
kiwi
lemons
mangoes
oranges
papaya
pineapple
pomegranates
raspberries
strawberries
tomatoes
watermelon

HERBS AND SPICES
allspice
basil
cilantro
cinnamon
clove
ginger
mint
oregano
parsley
rosemary
sage
thyme
turmeric

LEGUMES AND LENTILS
black beans
cannellini beans
garbanzo beans
kidney beans
lentils
pinto beans
soybeans
tofu

LOW-FAT DAIRY
kefir
low-fat milk
low-fat yogurt

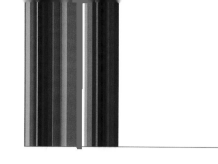

MEAT, FISH AND EGGS

cod

eggs

halibut

shrimp

skinless chicken breast

snapper

trout

tuna

wild salmon

NON-DAIRY BEVERAGES

almond milk

soymilk

NUTS AND SEEDS

almonds

flaxseed

hazelnuts

macadamia nuts

mustard seeds

pine nuts

sesame seeds

sunflower seeds

walnuts

OLIVES AND OILS

olive oil – cold-pressed extra-virgin

olives

walnut oil

TEAS

black tea

green tea

rooibos (red bush) tea

white tea

VEGETABLES

asparagus

beets

broccoli

broccoli rabe

Brussels sprouts

carrots

cauliflower

chili peppers

collard greens

green peppers

green-leaf lettuce

kale

mushrooms

pumpkin

red peppers

spinach

squash

sweet potato

yellow peppers

WHOLE GRAINS

barley

brown rice

buckwheat

millet

oatmeal

quinoa

whole wheat

wholewheat couscous

wholewheat pasta

AGE-DEFYING BENEFITS OF POWER FOODS

Power foods contain concentrated levels of many vitamins and nutrients that slow the aging process. I have listed some of the key anti-aging vitamins and nutrients, and foods that contain high amounts of these.

Beta-Carotene

A powerful antioxidant with anti-aging benefits. May prevent arthritis and skin cancer. The body converts it into vitamin A. Food sources of beta-carotene are recommended over supplements.

carrots	spinach
cilantro	squash
collard greens	sweet potatoes
kale	thyme

Coenzyme Q10

A powerhouse anti-aging antioxidant. It has extensive health benefits and slows aging of the skin, heart, and blood vessels.

broccoli	spinach
eggs	wheat germ
fish	whole grains
peanuts	

Flavonoids

Help protect cells from oxidative damage, inflammation, and enhance the antioxidant effect of vitamin C in the body, which promotes skin health and decreases irritating skin diseases.

apples	pinto beans
apricots	raspberries
black beans	strawberries
blueberries	tomatoes
onions	

Folic Acid

Helps promote cardiovascular and brain health as well as playing a role in skin cell production.

asparagus	lentils
black beans	spinach
garbanzo beans	

Lycopene

Helps prevent cell damage from free radicals. Assists in slowing the development of atherosclerosis (hardening of the arteries) and vision changes associated with macular degeneration.

apricots	tomatoes
papaya	watermelon
pink grapefruit	

Omega-3 Fatty Acids

Reduce inflammation throughout the body. Help lower cholesterol and triglyceride levels in the bloodstream, reducing the risk of cardiovascular disease. Important in promoting healthy skin, hair and nails.

flaxseed	tofu
halibut	walnuts
shrimp	wild salmon
soybeans	

Vitamin A — Beta-carotene in plant foods and retinol in animal foods

A great antioxidant that promotes healthy skin. Plays a role in the health of the immune system, bone growth and vision.

apricots	kale
basil	red peppers
broccoli	spinach
cantaloupe	squash
carrots	sweet potato
cilantro	thyme
collard greens	

Vitamin B

The B group of vitamins are vital to cell metabolism. They help promote healthy skin and muscle tone. They also help prevent depression and heart disease.

bananas	tuna
lentils	yogurt
sunflower seeds	

Vitamin C — Ascorbic acid

A key contributor to healthy skin. A great antioxidant that protects cells from free radical damage. Assists in iron absorption.

broccoli	lemons
Brussels sprouts	oranges
cabbage	papaya
cantaloupe	parsley
cauliflower	peppers
grapefruit	strawberries
green-leaf lettuce	tomatoes
kiwi	

Vitamin D and Calcium

Both are essential for the prevention of osteoporosis. Vitamin D reduces inflammation and age-related diseases such as hypertension and diabetes.

cod	sesame seeds
eggs	shrimp
milk	tuna
salmon	yogurt

Vitamin E — Tocopherol

One of the most powerful antioxidants, essential for beautiful skin. It protects against UV-induced skin damage and facilitates skin repair.

almonds	papaya
blueberries	red peppers
Brussels sprouts	spinach
eggs	sunflower seeds
kiwi	tomatoes
mustard greens	wholewheat bread
olives	

Breakfast

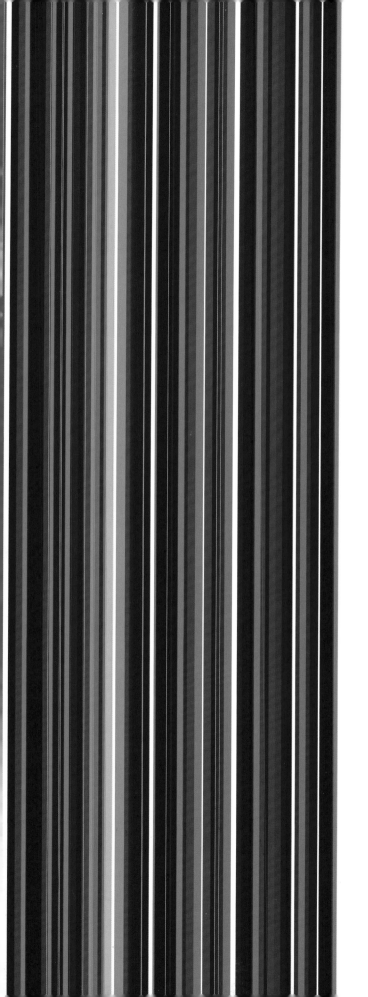

BREAKFAST

Papaya FRUIT SALAD

PREPARATION 15 mins

½ papaya, peeled

1 orange, peeled

2 kiwis, peeled

1 small banana, skin removed

¼ pineapple, skin removed

small bunch green grapes

small bunch red grapes

7 oz/200g strawberries

2 passion fruit, pulp only

2 sprigs mint leaves

juice of 1 lemon

2 tablespoons Grand Marnier
(optional)

1 Cut the papaya into small cubes, cut the orange into segments, cut kiwis into thin slices. Slice the banana into medium-size slices and dice the pineapple into cubes (do not use the pineapple core).

2 Gently combine all cut fruit with the grapes, strawberries and passion fruit pulp.

3 Separate the mint leaves and pour lemon juice over the fruit salad.

4 As an optional extra, pour over Grand Marnier. Scatter with mint leaves and serve as a centre-piece on a buffet table or in hearty individual serves.

The secret to this dish is the addition of lemon juice, which brings out the flavor of the payaya.

FRESH FRUIT *Salad*

serves 4

PREPARATION 1 hr 20 mins

---

2 oranges

3 tablespoons fresh, unsweetened orange juice

1 red apple, cut into medium-size pieces

1 pear, cut into medium-size pieces

2 oz/60g seedless grapes

1 nectarine, stoned and cut into chunks

1 banana

6 fresh strawberries

1 Slice the top and bottom off each orange and place on a work surface. Using a serrated knife, cut off the skin and pith, following the curves of the fruit. Holding the oranges over a bowl, cut between the membranes to release the segments. Put the segments into a large serving bowl with the orange juice.

2 Add the apple, pear, grapes and nectarine to the bowl and mix gently but thoroughly so that the orange juice coats the fruit (this will stop the fruit discoloring). Put the fruit salad in the refrigerator and chill for 1 hour to allow the flavors to develop.

3 Just before serving, peel the banana, slice it thinly and add to the bowl. Remove the green hulls from the strawberries, cut in half and add to the bowl. Mix gently and serve.

This is also good topped with some plain low-fat yogurt, a drizzle of honey and fresh mint sprigs.

Bircher **MUESLI**

serves 4

PREPARATION 1 hr 10 mins

1 apple, peeled and grated

1 pear, peeled and grated

2 cups rolled oats

½ teaspoon ground cinnamon

1 cup pear juice

5 oz/150g low-fat vanilla
yogurt

2 oz/60g toasted flaked
almonds

1 cup reduced-fat milk

2 mangoes, peeled and
chopped

1 banana, sliced

2 passion fruit or 2 kiwis,
finely chopped

1 Put the apple, pear, rolled oats,
cinnamon and pear juice in a bowl and
mix to combine. Allow to stand covered
in the refrigerator for 1 hour.

2 Remove from the refrigerator and fold
through the yogurt and almonds. Spoon
the muesli into individual bowls and serve
topped with the milk, mango and banana
and drizzled with passion fruit pulp or
chopped kiwi.

LAYERED FRUIT AND *yogurt* WITH BRAN

PREPARATION **10 mins**

3 oz/90g bran flakes

14 oz/400g low-fat Greek
yogurt

¼ cup honey

2 peaches, stoned and sliced

7 oz/200g strawberries,
halved

1 kiwi, sliced

2 small bananas, sliced

3 oz/90g organic raisins

1 Divide the bran equally among four
deep glasses. Top with yogurt, then drizzle
honey over the top.

2 Put the peaches, strawberries, kiwi
and bananas in a bowl and gently mix
to combine.

3 Spoon the fruit on top of the honey, then
finish off with a generous sprinkle of raisins.

FRESH FRUIT *Smoothie*

serves 4

PREPARATION 5 mins

2 cups mixed fruit, for
    example, strawberries,
    blueberries, mango pieces,
    papaya, apples

1 banana

¼ cup low-fat milk or soymilk

⅓ cup orange juice

½ cup crushed ice

1 Place glasses into the freezer to pre-chill.

2 Remove any green tops from fruits such as strawberries. Peel the banana and place all fruit in the blender.

3 Top with milk or soymilk, orange juice and crushed ice. Blend for 2 minutes, or until all ingredients are combined.

4 Pour into chilled glasses, top with extra pieces of sliced fruit and serve immedietly.

Peeling a banana and placing it in the freezer will create a wonderfully creamy and thick smoothie. You can omit the soymilk or milk and substitute a juice instead.

MUESLI/GRANOLA *Parfait*

2 cups plain low-fat yogurt

2 tablespoons honey

½ teaspoon cinnamon

½ cup muesli or granola

2 tablespoons walnuts or almonds, coarsely chopped

1½ cups chopped seasonal fruit, for example, blueberries, strawberries, apples, kiwi, peaches, mangoes, pears, peaches

2 sprigs mint to garnish

1 In a bowl, mix together yogurt, honey and cinnamon.

2 Divide half of the yogurt mixture between 4 tall clear glasses or parfait glasses. Add the muesli or granola, nuts and fruit. Cover with the remaining yogurt mixture.

3 Seperate the mint leaves and use as a garnish with a few fresh berries.

Buckwheat PANCAKES

serves 4

PREPARATION 5 mins
COOKING 10 mins

2 egg whites

½ cup buckwheat flour

½ cup wholewheat pastry
flour

¾ cup low-fat milk or soymilk

1 tablespoon safflower oil

2 teaspoons baking powder

½ teaspoon salt

1 tablespoon honey

1 Beat egg whites until fluffy. Add remaining ingredients and beat until just combined and smooth. Add additional milk or soymilk if a thinner batter is desired.

2 Lightly oil the griddle and heat. Test by sprinkling a few drops of water – if it bubbles, the heat is right.

3 For each pancake, pour approximately 3–4 tablespoons of batter onto the griddle. Cook until bubbles form. Turn and cook the other side briefly until golden brown.

4 Serve with real maple syrup.

Butternut PANCAKES

serves 4

PREPARATION **6 mins**
COOKING **10 mins**

2½ oz/75g butternut squash

1 egg, separated

1 tablespoon safflower oil

1 cup low-fat milk or soymilk

¼ cup applesauce

1½ cups wholewheat pastry
    flour

¼ teaspoon sea salt

½ teaspoon cinnamon

1½ teaspoons baking powder

maple syrup to serve

fresh fruit to serve

1 Cut the butternut squash into large cubes and steam for 5 minutes until soft, then cool.

2 Beat egg white until stiff. In a separate bowl, beat egg yolk, oil, butternut squash, milk and applesauce.

3 In another bowl, sift the remaining dry ingredients, then stir in the butternut mixture. Gently fold in the egg white.

4 Lightly oil the griddle and heat. Test by sprinkling a few drops of water – if it bubbles, the heat is right. For each pancake, pour approximately 3–4 tablespoons of batter onto griddle. When bubbles appear on top of the pancakes, turn and cook until the other side has just become brown.

5 Serve with real maple syrup and fresh seasonal fruit.

Wholewheat **WAFFLES**

serves 4

PREPARATION 6 mins

COOKING 10 mins

½ cup wholewheat pastry
flour

½ cup wholewheat flour

2 egg whites

1 ½ tablespoons safflower oil

2 tablespoons applesauce

2 tablespoons honey

¼ teaspoon salt

2 teaspoons baking powder

⅔ cup water

1 tablespoon soymilk

fresh fruit to serve

maple syrup to serve

1 Mix all ingredients except fruit and maple
syrup until just combined.

2 Heat waffle iron. Pour in batter until
almost full, close and cook for approximately
4 minutes or until golden brown.

3 Serve with fresh fruit of your choice.
Drizzle with real maple syrup.

CLASSIC HERB *Omelette*

serves 4

| PREPARATION 5 mins |
| COOKING 15 mins |

4 large eggs

8 large egg whites

salt and black pepper

4 teaspoons extra-virgin olive oil

8 tablespoons freshly chopped mixed herbs, such as cilantro, parsley and chives

1 For each omelette, crack 1 whole egg into a small bowl, add 2 egg whites, then season. Mix lightly with a fork for about 20 seconds, until just blended.

2 Place a small non-stick skillet over a high heat. When hot, add 1 teaspoon of the oil and tilt the pan until it covers the base.

3 Pour the eggs into the pan, then tilt the pan so that they cover the base and start to set. After about 10 seconds, use a wooden spatula to pull the cooked egg gently from the edge of the pan towards the centre, so that any uncooked egg runs underneath and sets. Continue pulling the edges until all the egg has set (this will take 2–3 minutes).

4 Sprinkle a quarter of the herbs evenly over the omelette and season with more salt and pepper. Then, using the spatula, gently fold the omelette in half. Tilt the pan and slide the omelette onto a plate if serving immediately, or keep warm in a low oven while preparing additional omelettes.

Try these variations: sprinkle 1 oz/30g of crumbled low-fat feta over the omelette just before folding, or heat 2 teaspoons of extra-virgin olive oil in a small skillet over a gentle heat, add 2 oz/60g finely sliced button mushrooms and cook for 3–4 minutes, stirring, until softened, then spread over the omelette just before serving.

Soups

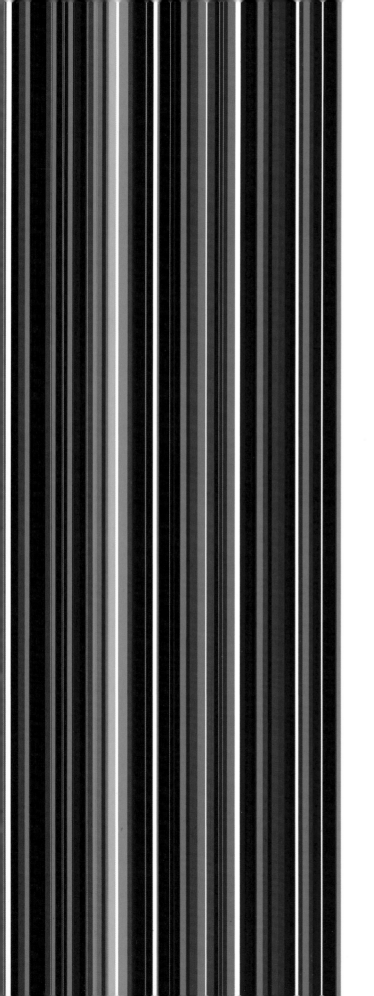

SOUPS

TOMATO *Ginger* SOUP

serves 4

2 tablespoons extra-virgin olive oil

1 large sweet onion, chopped

2 carrots, peeled and diced

2 sticks celery, chopped

2 cloves garlic, minced

½ in/1cm piece fresh ginger, finely chopped

3 teaspoons fennel seeds, toasted in dry skillet for 2 minutes then crushed

½ fennel bulb, chopped (save leaves for garnish)

1 teaspoon sea salt

2 x 14 oz/400g canned crushed tomatoes

3 cups vegetable bouillon

freshly ground black pepper

¼ cup chopped fresh cilantro

1 Heat oil in heavy saucepan. Add onion and sauté on medium heat until translucent.

2 Add carrots, celery, garlic, fresh ginger, crushed fennel seeds, fresh fennel bulb and sea salt. Simmer until soft, approximately 5–10 minutes.

3 Add tomatoes, stir and cook briefly. Add vegetable bouillon. Bring to a boil, stirring constantly. Cover and simmer for 20 minutes.

4 Place small amounts in a blender or food processor and blend until smooth. Return to saucepan. Add fresh ground pepper, and cilantro. Stir and serve.

Japanese **NOODLE SOUP WITH FRESH TUNA**

serves 4

PREPARATION **5 mins**

COOKING **20 mins**

2¼ cups fish bouillon

4 tablespoons dark soy sauce

4 tablespoons sake or
 dry sherry

2 tablespoons rice or
 wine vinegar

1 tablespoon honey

2 tablespoons sesame oil

9 oz/250g soba noodles

4 tuna steaks, about
 5 oz/150g each, skinned

2 tablespoons sesame seeds

fresh cilantro to garnish

1 Put the bouillon, soy sauce, sake or sherry, vinegar, honey and 1 tablespoon of the oil into a saucepan. Bring to the boil and cook, uncovered, for 15 minutes or until reduced by about a third.

2 Meanwhile, prepare the noodles according to the packet instructions, until tender but still firm to the bite. Brush the tuna steaks with the remaining oil and coat the edges with sesame seeds.

3 Heat a ridged cast-iron grill pan or heavy-based skillet until very hot. Add the tuna steaks and cook for 2 minutes on each side or until seared.

4 Transfer the noodles to serving bowls, pour over the bouillon, top with the tuna steaks and garnish with cilantro, then serve immediately.

SPICED FISH, TOMATO AND *Garbanzo* SOUP

serves 4

PREPARATION 15 mins

COOKING 35 mins

1 tablespoon extra-virgin olive oil

1 onion, chopped

1 teaspoon ground cilantro

1 teaspoon ground cumin

1 teaspoon ground turmeric

1 teaspoon allspice

1 green chili, finely sliced

14 oz/400g canned chopped tomatoes

14 oz/400g canned garbanzo beans, rinsed and drained

3 cups reduced-salt fish bouillon

9 oz/250g firm white fish fillets (cod, halibut, red snapper), cut into large pieces

⅓ cup wholewheat couscous

¼ cup thick, low-fat plain yogurt

1 tablespoon chopped fresh parsley

1 tablespoon chopped fresh mint

1 Heat the oil in a large pot, add the onion and cook over a medium heat for 3 minutes or until the onion is soft and golden.

2 Add the spices and chili and cook until fragrant, about 2 minutes. Stir in the tomatoes, garbanzo beans and fish bouillon and bring to the boil. Reduce the heat and simmer uncovered for 15 minutes.

3 Add the fish and cook for 5 minutes or until the fish is just tender. Remove the soup from the heat, then add the couscous and cover. Set aside for 10 minutes or until the couscous is soft. Stir and ladle into serving bowls.

4 Serve with a dollop of yogurt and sprinkle with parsley and mint. Accompany with warmed wholewheat pita bread.

CUMIN-SPICED *Carrot* SOUP

serves 4

PREPARATION 15 mins

COOKING 40 mins

1 tablespoon extra-virgin olive oil

1 large onion, chopped

1 clove garlic, crushed

3 sticks celery, chopped

1 tablespoon ground cumin

24 oz/680g carrots, thinly sliced

4 cups vegetable bouillon

sea salt

black pepper

1 Heat the oil in a large saucepan. Add the onion, garlic, and celery and fry gently for 5 minutes or until softened, stirring occasionally. Add the cumin and fry, stirring, for 1 minute to release its flavor.

2 Add the carrots, bouillon, salt and pepper and stir to combine. Bring to the boil and simmer, covered, for 30–35 minutes until the vegetables are tender, stirring occasionally.

3 Remove the pan from the heat and cool for a few minutes. Purée the soup until smooth in a food processor, liquidizer, or with a hand blender. Return to a clean pan and reheat gently. Serve with wholewheat toast and garnished with fresh cilantro.

This thick soup will really warm you up on a cold winter's night. To get the best flavor, spend a bit extra on fresh bouillon.

SPINACH AND *Almond* SOUP

serves 4

PREPARATION 5 mins

COOKING 10 mins

18 oz/500g baby spinach

3½ cups vegetable bouillon

3½ oz/100g ground almonds

sea salt and black pepper

½ cup fat-free evaporated
    milk

2 oz/60g grated Parmesan
    cheese

1 Put the spinach into a large saucepan with the bouillon, reserving a few leaves to garnish. Bring to the boil, then reduce the heat and simmer for 5 minutes. Stir in the almonds and seasoning and simmer for 2 minutes. Remove from the heat and leave to cool a little.

2 Pour into a food processor and blend to a smooth purée, or use a hand blender. Add the evaporated milk, return to the pan and reheat gently – don't let the soup boil.

3 Serve topped with the Parmesan and a sprinkling of pepper, and garnished with the reserved spinach.

Not only do the almonds add their distinctive taste to this spinach soup, they also give it a lovely thick texture. It's delicious hot or cold, especially if you use fresh bouillon.

CARIBBEAN *Gazpacho* WITH AVOCADO SALSA

serves 4

PREPARATION **12 mins**

½ cucumber, finely diced

¼ pineapple, finely diced

½ mango, finely diced

¼ red pepper, finely diced

2 plum tomatoes, finely diced

1 green onion, chopped

2 tablespoons freshly chopped mint

2 tablespoons freshly chopped cilantro

1 cup tomato or vegetable juice

1 cup pineapple juice

1 teaspoon no-added-salt Worcestershire sauce

Tabasco sauce

sea salt and freshly ground black pepper

AVOCADO SALSA

1 avocado, diced

1 tablespoon freshly chopped cilantro

sea salt and black pepper

1 teaspoon lime juice

1 Place the cucumber, pineapple, mango, red pepper, tomatoes, green onion, mint, cilantro, tomato juice, pineapple juice and Worcestershire sauce in a glass bowl. Add a dash of Tobasco and mix to combine. Cover and refrigerate overnight or until cold. Season to taste with salt and pepper.

2 To serve, ladle the soup into chilled bowls. Top with a spoonful of salsa.

AVOCADO SALSA

1 Place the avocado, cilantro, salt, pepper and lime juice in a bowl and mix to combine. Cover and refrigerate until ready to use. The salsa is best used within a few days.

YELLOW PEPPER SOUP WITH
RED PEPPER *Harissa*

serves 4

PREPARATION 15 mins

COOKING 30 mins

2 teaspoons extra-virgin olive oil

3 yellow peppers, diced

1 carrot, finely diced

1 small onion, diced

1 medium sweet potato, diced

2 cups hot reduced-salt vegetable or chicken bouillon

zest of 1 orange, grated

juice of 1 orange

freshly ground black pepper

RED PEPPER HARISSA

2 red peppers, cut in half lengthwise, seeds removed

2 tomatoes, cut in half

1 tablespoon red wine vinegar

2 teaspoons no-added-salt tomato paste

hot chili sauce

sea salt and freshly ground black pepper

flat-leaf parsley to garnish

1 Heat the oil in a non-stick saucepan over a low heat. Add the yellow peppers, carrot and onion. Cook, stirring, for 10 minutes or until the peppers are soft. Add the sweet potato and bouillon. Simmer for 20 minutes or until the potato is soft. Cool slightly.

2 Transfer mixture to a food processor. Add orange zest and juice and purée. Season with black pepper. Return soup to a clean saucepan. Reheat.

3 To serve, ladle soup into warm bowls and top with harissa.

HARISSA

1 Preheat grill to hot. Using your hands, gently flatten the red pepper and tomato halves and place, skin-side up, on aluminum foil under the grill. Cook until skins blacken. Set aside until cool enough to handle. Remove skins.

2 Place pepper and tomato flesh in a food processor. Add vinegar, tomato paste, hot chili sauce, salt and black pepper. Purée and set aside until ready to serve.

3 Serve with a sprig of flat-leaf parsley.

Watercress SOUP

serves 4

PREPARATION 35 mins
COOKING 30 mins

1 tablespoon extra-virgin
   olive oil

4 spring onions, finely
   chopped

1 leek, thinly sliced

9 oz/250g potatoes, diced

1 cup watercress, chopped

2 cups vegetable bouillon

2 cups low-fat milk

sea salt

black pepper, coarsely
   ground

1 Heat the oil in a large saucepan, then add the spring onions and leek and cook gently for 5 minutes or until softened, stirring occasionally. Add the potatoes and watercress and cook for a further 3 minutes or until the watercress wilts, stirring occasionally.

2 Stir in the bouillon, milk, sea salt and pepper. Bring to a boil, then reduce the heat and simmer, covered, for 20 minutes or until the potatoes are cooked and tender, stirring occasionally.

3 Remove the pan from the heat and cool for a few minutes. Purée the soup until smooth in a food processor, liquidizer, or with a hand blender. Return to a clean pan and reheat gently, until piping hot. Serve seasoned with black pepper.

This quick soup is full of goodness but it looks and tastes sophisticated enough to serve at any dinner party. For a change, use chopped spinach instead of watercress.

Roasted **TOMATO, RED PEPPER AND BREAD SOUP**

serves 4

PREPARATION 10 mins
COOKING 60 mins

2 lb/1kg plum tomatoes

2 red peppers

3 tablespoons extra-virgin olive oil

3 cloves garlic, crushed

2 onions, finely chopped

2 teaspoons ground cumin

1 teaspoon turmeric

1 teaspoon ground cilantro

4 cups vegetable or chicken bouillon

2 slices wholewheat bread, crusts removed and torn into pieces

1 tablespoon balsamic vinegar

sea salt and freshly ground black pepper

1 Preheat the oven to 440°F/220°C.

2 Place the tomatoes and peppers in a lightly oiled baking dish and bake for 20 minutes or until the skins have blistered. Set aside to cool, then remove the skins and roughly chop.

3 Heat the oil in a saucepan, add the garlic and onion and cook for 5 minutes, or until soft. Add the cumin, turmeric and cilantro, and cook for 1 minute until well combined. Add tomatoes, peppers and bouillon to the saucepan, bring to the boil and simmer for 30 minutes. Add bread, balsamic vinegar and salt and pepper, and cook for a further 5–10 minutes.

4 Serve with fresh cilantro and Parmesan cheese, if desired.

THAI *Spiked* PUMPKIN SOUP

serves 4

PREPARATION 8 mins

COOKING 2 hrs

2 tablespoons extra-virgin olive oil

1 large brown onion

4 cloves garlic

1 small red bird's-eye chili

½ bunch cilantro

½ teaspoon chili paste

1 teaspoon ground cumin

1 teaspoon turmeric

13 oz/370g butternut squash

13 oz/370g acorn squash

13 oz/370g pumpkin

4 cups vegetable bouillon

14 fl oz/400mL coconut milk

1 Heat the olive oil in a large saucepan and add the onion and garlic and cook for 10 minutes to gently caramelize. Finely chop the cilantro roots and bird's-eye chili, add to the pan and stir until fragrant.

2 Add the remaining spices and heat until toasted. Add all the squash and pumpkin pieces and stir to coat with the spice mixture. Cover with a lid and cook over a low heat for 30 minutes until the pumpkin is beginning to soften and turn brown. Add just enough bouillon to cover, and stir well.

3 Simmer for 1 hour, then add the coconut milk and simmer for a further 15 minutes. Purée then serve, garnished with extra chilies and cilantro leaves.

SWEET POTATO, *Couscous* AND LEEK SOUP

serves 4

PREPARATION	20 mins
COOKING	40 mins

2 teaspoons extra-virgin olive oil

2 small leeks, thinly sliced

pinch of saffron

21 oz/600g sweet potato, peeled and chopped

6 cups reduced-salt chicken or vegetable bouillon

1 cinnamon stick

1 teaspoon ground cinnamon

½ teaspoon turmeric

1 bouquet garni

1 cup wholewheat couscous

2 cups boiling water

½ cup raisins

2 tablespoons chopped fresh chives

PITA CRISPS

2 wholewheat pita breads

1 tablespoon extra-virgin olive oil

1 oz/30g Parmesan cheese, finely grated

1 Heat the oil in a large pot, add the leeks and cook over a medium heat for 5 minutes or until the leeks are soft and golden. Add the saffron and sweet potato and stir for about 5 minutes or until the sweet potato begins to soften.

2 Stir in the bouillon, cinnamon stick and ground cinnamon, turmeric and bouquet garni. Bring to the boil then reduce the heat and simmer for 30 minutes, or until the sweet potato is very soft. Remove the cinnamon stick and bouquet garni.

3 Place couscous in a large bowl. Add boiling water. Cover for 10 minutes. Remove cover and fluff with a fork. Set aside.

4 Purée the soup in batches until smooth, then return to the pot along with the couscous and reheat gently. If it is too thick, add a little water. Add the raisins and stir to mix through.

5 To make the pita crisps, use a star-shaped cookie cutter to cut out shapes from the pita bread, brush lightly with oil, sprinkle with Parmesan cheese and place another star on top. Grill until crisp and golden.

6 To serve, ladle the soup into bowls, float pita stars on top and sprinkle with chives.

CURRIED *Lentil* SOUP

serves 4

PREPARATION 15 mins
COOKING 65 mins

2 tablespoons extra-virgin olive oil

1 onion, chopped

2 teaspoons curry powder

½ teaspoon turmeric

½ teaspoon ground cumin

2 teaspoons tomato paste

34 fl oz/1 litre vegetable bouillon

30 oz/90g red or green lentils

1 small head broccoli, broken into florets

1 carrot, chopped

1 parsnip, chopped

1 stalk celery, chopped

freshly ground black pepper

sea salt

1 tablespoon chopped fresh parsley

1 Heat oil in a large saucepan, add onion, curry powder, turmeric and cumin and cook, stirring occasionally, for 4–5 minutes or until onion is soft. Stir in tomato paste and bouillon and bring to the boil. Reduce heat, add lentils, cover and simmer for 30 minutes.

2 Add broccoli, carrots, parsnip and celery and cook, covered, for 30 minutes longer or until vegetables are tender.

3 Season to taste with black pepper and sea salt. Just prior to serving, stir in parsley.

Porcini MUSHROOM SOUP

serves 4

PREPARATION	10 mins
COOKING	50 mins

1 tablespoon dried porcini

½ cup boiling water

2 tablespoons extra-virgin
   olive oil

2 cloves garlic, minced

1 leek, chopped

6 shallots, chopped

7 oz/200g white mushrooms

13 oz/370g forest
   mushrooms, for example,
   porcini, shiitake and oyster

2 tablespoons wholewheat
   pastry flour

3 cups good-quality chicken
   or vegetable bouillon

1 cup fat-free evaporated milk

½ bunch chopped flat-leaf
   parsley

20 basil leaves, sliced

1 tablespoon fresh oregano

sea salt and pepper

1 Add the dried porcini to the boiling water and set aside. When the mushrooms have softened, remove them from the mushroom water and set aside. Strain the mushroom liquid through a paper towel or muslin-lined sieve to remove sand and grit, and reserve the liquid.

2 Heat the olive oil and add the garlic, leeks and shallots and cook until golden, about 3 minutes. Thinly slice all the fresh mushrooms, add to the pan, and cook over a very high heat until the mushrooms soften and their liquid evaporates, about 6 minutes. Reserve a few mushroom pieces for a garnish.

3 Sprinkle with the flour and stir well to enable the flour to be absorbed. Add the bouillon and the porcini mushrooms together with the soaking liquid and bring to the boil, stirring frequently.

4 Once the soup is boiling, reduce the heat to a simmer and cook for 30 minutes. Add the evaporated milk and simmer for a further 5 minutes or until slightly thickened. Add half the chopped parsley, the sliced basil and oregano and season to taste with salt and pepper.

5 To serve, ladle into individual bowls, sprinkle with extra parsley, reserved mushrooms, a little nutmeg and a small drizzle of extra cream if desired.

TOMATO, LENTIL AND *Basil* SOUP

6 tablespoons lentils

2 lb/1kg plum tomatoes

1 tablespoon extra-virgin olive oil

2 onions, chopped

2 tablespoons sun-dried tomato purée

3 cups vegetable bouillon

1 bay leaf

sea salt

black pepper

3 tablespoons chopped fresh basil, plus extra leaves to garnish

1 Rinse the lentils, drain, then add them to a large saucepan of boiling water. Simmer, uncovered, for 25 minutes or until tender. Drain, rinse and set aside.

2 Meanwhile, place the tomatoes in a bowl, cover with boiling water, leave for 30 seconds, then drain. Remove the skins, deseed and chop.

3 Heat the oil in a large saucepan, add the onions and cook for 10 minutes or until softened, stirring occasionally. Stir in the tomatoes, tomato purée, bouillon, bay leaf, sea salt and pepper. Bring to the boil and simmer, covered, stirring occasionally, for 25 minutes or until all the vegetables are cooked.

4 Remove the pan from the heat and cool for a few minutes. Remove and discard the bay leaf, then purée the soup until smooth in a food processor, liquidizer, or with a hand blender. Return to a clean pan, stir in the lentils and chopped basil, then reheat gently. Serve garnished with the fresh basil.

GARBANZO, *Roasted* TOMATO AND GARLIC SOUP

serves 4

PREPARATION	15 mins
COOKING	1 hr 40 mins

18 oz/500g dried garbanzo beans

2 lb/1kg plum tomatoes

1 bulb garlic

¼ cup extra-virgin olive oil

sea salt

2 tablespoons dried oregano

2 leeks, sliced, white part only

4 cups chicken or vegetable bouillon

2 tablespoons tomato paste

freshly ground black pepper

fresh oregano leaves

1 Soak garbanzo beans in cold water overnight. Drain, then place in a saucepan covered with fresh water and bring to the boil, then simmer for approximately 1 hour until cooked. Drain and set aside.

2 Preheat the oven to 400°F/200°C. Halve the tomatoes and place them in a baking tray. Cut the top off the garlic bulb and place it in the baking tray.

3 Drizzle with a little olive oil, sprinkle with salt and dried oregano, and roast in the oven for 20–30 minutes.

4 Place the tomatoes and 5 peeled garlic cloves in a food processor, and purée for 1 minute. Reserve the remaining garlic cloves for later use – they are especially good as a spread on toast.

5 Heat half the oil and sauté the leeks for 3 minutes. Add the bouillon and bring to the boil, then reduce heat to a simmer.

6 Add the tomato mixture, tomato paste and garbanzo beans, season with salt and pepper, and heat through.

7 Sprinkle with fresh oregano leaves just before serving.

THICK *Minestrone* WITH PESTO

serves *4*

PREPARATION **20** mins

COOKING **45** mins

3 tablespoons extra-virgin olive oil

1 onion, chopped

2 cloves garlic

1 potato, skin on, cut into 1cm cubes

2 small carrots, cut into 1cm cubes

1 large zucchini, cut into 1cm cubes

¼ white cabbage, chopped

3 cups vegetable bouillon

2 x 14 oz/400g canned chopped tomatoes

3 oz/90g wholewheat pasta shapes, such as conchiglie shells

sea salt and black pepper

2 oz/60g Parmesan cheese, grated

4 tablespoons pesto

1 Heat the oil in a large heavy-based saucepan, then add the onion, garlic, potato, carrots, zucchini and cabbage and cook for 5–7 minutes, until slightly softened.

2 Add the bouillon and tomatoes and bring to the boil. Reduce the heat and simmer for 20 minutes, then add the pasta and seasoning and cook for a further 15 minutes or until the pasta is tender but still firm to the bite.

3 Divide the soup between bowls, top each with a tablespoon each of Parmesan and pesto and serve.

MINESTRONE *Piemonte*

serves 4

PREPARATION	15 mins
COOKING	2 hrs 40 mins

½ cup small white beans

½ cup kidney beans

½ cup garbanzo beans

4 white onions, chopped

2 cloves garlic, minced

3 tablespoons olive oil

½ small cabbage, sliced

2 sticks celery, sliced

2 medium carrots,
   finely sliced

6 cups good-quality vegetable
   or chicken bouillon

2 tablespoons tomato paste

12 basil leaves, chopped

6 sprigs parsley

3 bay leaves (fresh if possible)

sea salt and pepper

3½ oz/100g piece Parmesan
   rind

4 zucchini, sliced

1 cup red wine

1 The night before, mix the white, kidney and garbanzo beans together and soak in cold water. If you don't have time to soak the beans overnight, cover them with hot water for 2 hours then drain and proceed with the recipe.

2 Sauté the onions and garlic in the olive oil for 5 minutes or until soft. Add the cabbage, celery and carrots and sauté for a further 5 minutes or until the vegetables have softened.

3 Add the bouillon, tomato paste, bean mixture, basil, parsley, bay leaves and salt and pepper and simmer for 2 hours or until thick and fragrant.

4 Add the Parmesan rind, zucchini, wine and a little extra water if necessary to thin the soup. Cook for a further 30 minutes, remove bay leaves and Parmesan rind and serve.

A particularly nice touch is to finish each bowl with a spoonful of pesto. The heat of the soup warms the pesto and allows it to permeate throughout the entire bowl of soup.

MIXED *Bean* SOUP

serves 4

PREPARATION 8 mins
COOKING 1 hr 20 mins

3 oz/90g dried kidney beans

3 oz/90g dried cannellini beans

2 tablespoons extra-virgin olive oil

1 onion, chopped

1 clove garlic, crushed

3 stalks celery, sliced

2 carrots, chopped

2 potatoes, chopped

6 cups chicken or vegetable bouillon

14 oz/400g canned tomatoes, undrained and mashed

¼ cabbage, finely shredded

2 oz/60g small wholewheat pasta shapes or brown rice

1 teaspoon dried mixed herbs

freshly ground black pepper

Parmesan cheese, finely shaved

fresh basil and oregano

1 Place kidney and cannellini beans in a bowl. Cover with cold water and set aside to soak overnight. Drain.

2 Heat oil in a saucepan over a medium heat, add onion and garlic and cook, stirring, for 5 minutes or until onion is tender. Add celery, carrots and potatoes and cook for 1 minute longer.

3 Stir in the bouillon, tomatoes, cabbage, pasta or rice, kidney and cannellini beans, herbs and black pepper and bring to the boil. Boil for 10 minutes, then reduce the heat and simmer, stirring occasionally, for 1 hour or until the beans are tender.

4 Sprinkle with Parmesan cheese and fresh basil and oregano and serve.

Curried **CREAM OF VEGETABLE SOUP**

serves 4

| PREPARATION | 20 mins |
| COOKING | 30 mins |

4 tablespoons extra-virgin
olive oil

3 tablespoons curry powder

1 teaspoon ground cinnamon

1 teaspoon nutmeg

1 teaspoon turmeric

1 teaspoon ground ginger

3 carrots, diced

2 onions, chopped

2 cloves garlic, chopped

2 sweet potatoes, diced

2 zucchini, diced

4 cups vegetable bouillon

15 oz/425g canned
cannellini beans, rinsed
and drained

15 oz/425g canned red
kidney beans, rinsed
and drained

¾ cup low-fat sour cream
or crème fraîche

sea salt

2 teaspoons chopped fresh
Italian parsley

1 Place the oil in a large heavy-based saucepan. Add the curry powder, cinnamon, nutmeg, turmeric and ginger and cook for 1 minute, then add the carrots, onions, garlic, potatoes and zucchini. Stir to coat thoroughly in the oil and spice mixture and cook for a further 5 minutes.

2 Add the bouillon and bring to the boil. Reduce the heat and simmer for 20 minutes or until the vegetables are tender. Add the cannellini and red kidney beans and gently heat through.

3 Remove from the heat and stir in the sour cream or crème fraîche. Season to taste and serve sprinkled with parsley. Serve with warm wholegrain bread.

A dollop of sour cream or crème fraîche makes a creamy contrast to the spicy flavor of this versatile soup.

Tuscan **BEAN AND BREAD SOUP**

serves 4

PREPARATION 10 mins
COOKING 20 mins

½ loaf wholewheat ciabatta bread or other wholewheat Italian bread

2 tablespoons extra-virgin olive oil

3 onions, chopped

3 cloves garlic, chopped

2 x 14 oz/400g canned chopped tomatoes

15 oz/425g canned cannellini beans, rinsed and drained

2½ cups vegetable bouillon

sea salt and black pepper

basil leaves to garnish

1 Preheat the oven to 300°F/150°C. Cut the bread into cubes, then place in the oven for 10 minutes to dry out.

2 Heat the oil in a large saucepan, add the onions and garlic, and cook for 3–4 minutes, until soft. Add the tomatoes, beans and bouillon, bring to the boil, then simmer for 2 minutes.

3 Stir in the bread cubes, bring soup back to the boil, then simmer for a further 5 minutes. Season, then serve garnished with basil.

Dee Dee's FRENCH PUMPKIN SOUP

serves 4

PREPARATION 10 mins
COOKING 30 mins

2 tablespoons extra-virgin olive oil

1 large onion, peeled and diced

2 carrots, peeled and chopped

2 sticks celery, chopped

1 clove garlic, crushed

500g pumpkin or butternut squash, chopped

2 x 14 oz/400g canned peeled whole tomatoes

1 teaspoon dried oregano

1 teaspoon dried basil

1 teaspoon ground cinnamon

1 teaspoon turmeric

2 teaspoons sea salt

4 cups vegetable bouillon

freshly ground black pepper

4 teaspoons low-fat sour cream

chopped fresh chives

1 Heat olive oil in a heavy-based saucepan. Add onions and sauté over medium heat until translucent. Add carrots, celery, garlic and cook until soft. Add the pumpkin or squash, tomatoes, oregano, basil, cinnamon, turmeric and sea salt and toss until combined. Add vegetable bouillon.

2 Bring to a boil and simmer, covered, for approximately 25 minutes or until pumpkin or squash is soft.

3 Purée soup in batches. Return to pan over low heat. Add black pepper.

4 Ladle into serving bowls and garnish with a teaspoon of sour cream and a sprinkling of chives.

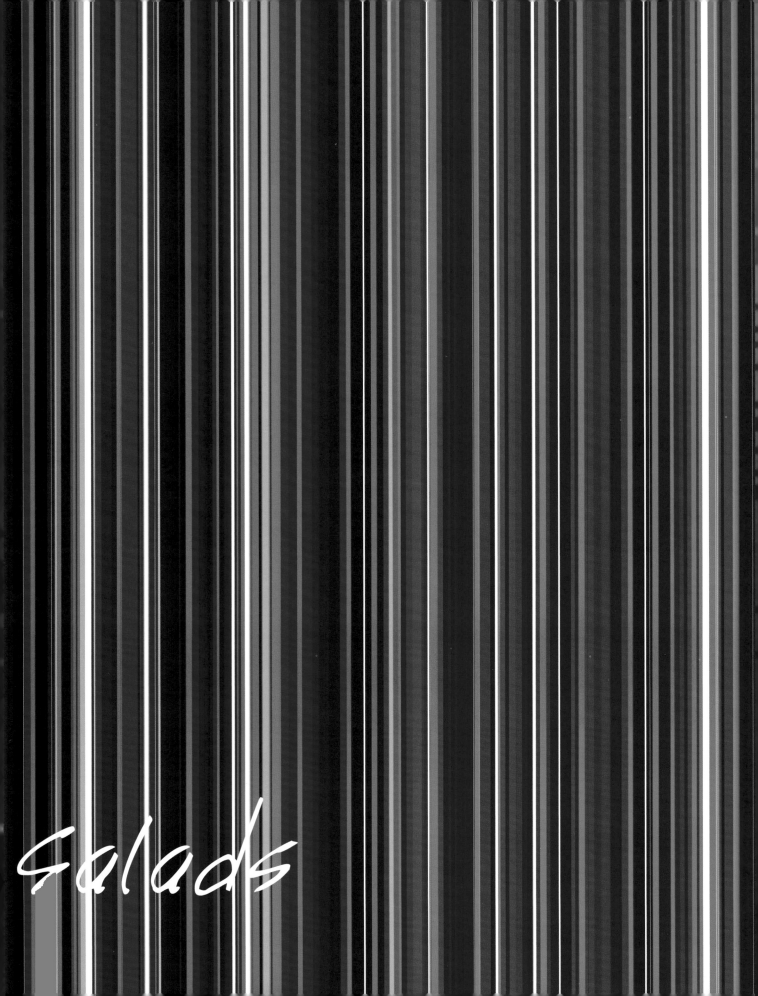

Salads

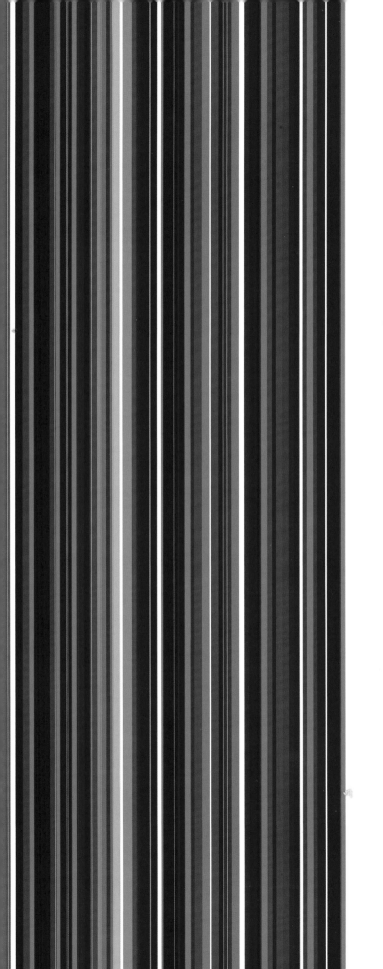

SALADS

MELON *Papaya* SALAD

serves 4

PREPARATION 5 mins

½ watermelon

½ honeydew melon

1 papaya

juice of 1 lime

zest of ½ lime

¼ teaspoon sea salt

½ teaspoon chili powder

2 tablespoons fresh mint

1 Cut the watermelon into medium-size cubes, removing all skin in the process.

2 Cut the honeydew melon into smaller cubes, removing all skin.

3 Cut the papaya into even smaller cubes, again removing all of the skin in the process. Combine all of the fruit with the lime juice and zest.

4 Combine the sea salt and chili powder in a small bowl. Sprinkle the fruit with half the salt and chili mixture and gently toss to combine. Tear pieces of mint and scatter over the salad. Serve in a large bowl or as individual portions. Sprinkle remaining chili salt mixture over salad just before serving.

A small amount of raw sugar may also be added to the spice mixture to give this recipe a more Thai-style flavor.

POMEGRANATE *Exotica*

2 avocados

juice of ½ lime

2 papayas

2 oz/60g mixed salad leaves

¾ cup pomegranate seeds

fresh cilantro to garnish

DRESSING

1 mango

1 tablespoon rice wine
   vinegar

juice of 1 lime

½ teaspoon extra-virgin
   olive oil

½ in/1cm piece ginger,
   peeled and finely chopped

½ teaspoon honey

1 Halve and peel the avocados, discarding the stones, then finely slice lengthwise. Gently toss in the lime juice in a large bowl.

2 Halve the papayas, then scoop out and discard the seeds. Peel and finely slice the flesh. Add to the avocado, then add the salad leaves and gently toss to combine.

3 To make the dressing, peel the mango, slice the flesh off the stone, then chop roughly. Blend to a thin purée with the vinegar, lime juice, oil, ginger and honey in a food processor.

4 Serve as individual side salads topped with the dressing and garnished with pomegranate seeds and cilantro leaves.

Roasted VEGETABLE SALAD

serves 4

PREPARATION 15 mins
COOKING 35 mins

3½ oz/100g broccoli florets

12 asparagus spears, trimmed

3 red onions, quartered

3 sweet potatoes, scrubbed and cut into wedges

2 zucchini, thickly sliced

2 yellow peppers, thickly sliced

4 tomatoes, halved

2 tablespoons extra-virgin olive oil

sea salt and freshly ground black pepper

shaved Parmesan cheese

DRESSING

3 tablespoons extra-virgin olive oil

2 tablespoons honey

1 tablespoon balsamic vinegar

finely grated zest and juice of ½ lemon

1 Preheat the oven to 400°F/200°C. Place all the vegetables in a shallow roasting tin, drizzle over the olive oil and season. Shake the tray gently to coat the vegetables well.

2 Bake for about 35 minutes, until the vegetables are very tender and slightly charred at the edges.

3 Mix all the dressing ingredients together and pour over the roasted vegetables. Toss well and divide onto 4 plates. Top with Parmesan. Serve with plenty of fresh, crusty bread to soak up the dressing.

This salad combines a healthy mix of the antioxidant vitamins A, C, and E, plus loads of minerals from the great-tasting vegetables. Remember, the more brightly-colored the vegetables, the more nutrients they are likely to contain. Roasting brings out vegetables' flavor and intensifies their natural sweetness.

MARINATED *Mushrooms* ON A BED OF LEAVES

serves 4

PREPARATION 2 hrs

3 tablespoons extra-virgin olive oil

2 tablespoons unsweetened apple juice

2 teaspoons tarragon white wine vinegar

2 teaspoons Dijon mustard

1 clove garlic, crushed

1 teaspoon chopped fresh mixed herbs, such as oregano, thyme, chives, basil and parsley

sea salt

freshly ground black pepper

4 cups mixed mushrooms, such as shiitake, large open, button and oyster, thickly sliced

9 oz/250g baby spinach leaves

1 oz/30g watercress, thick stems discarded

fresh thyme to garnish

1 Place the oil, apple juice, vinegar, mustard, garlic, herbs, salt and pepper in a bowl and whisk with a fork to mix thoroughly.

2 Pour the marinade over the mushrooms and stir well. Cover and place in the refrigerator for 2 hours.

3 Arrange the spinach and watercress on serving plates. Spoon the mushrooms and a little of the marinade over the top and toss lightly to mix. Garnish with the fresh thyme.

The longer you leave the mushrooms the more they will absorb the flavors of the tangy mustard dressing.

GRILLED *Brie* WITH BEET SALAD

PREPARATION 15 mins

COOKING 10 mins

1 avocado

9 oz/250g cooked beets, drained and chopped

2 celery sticks, sliced

1 red dessert apple, cored and chopped

4 slices wholewheat bread

4½ oz/125g Dutch Brie or goat's cheese, quartered

4½ oz/125g mixed salad leaves

DRESSING

3 tablespoons extra-virgin olive oil

3 tablespoons cider vinegar

1 clove garlic, crushed

1 small red onion, finely chopped

1 tablespoon tomato purée

sea salt and freshly ground black pepper

1 Peel and slice the avocado and place in a bowl together with the beets, celery and apple. Cover and set aside.

2 Preheat the grill to high and lightly toast the bread for 2–3 minutes each side. Place a slice of Brie or goat's cheese on top of each piece of toast, then return them to the grill. Cook until the cheese is melted and slightly golden.

3 Meanwhile, make the dressing. Place all the ingredients in a small saucepan and bring to the boil. Simmer for 2–3 minutes, until warmed through.

4 To serve, divide the salad leaves between 4 plates, top with the beet mixture and place a piece of cheese toast on each plate. Drizzle over the warm dressing and serve immediately.

Cherry TOMATO SALAD

serves 4

2 cups cherry tomatoes

9 oz/250g feta cheese

2 green onions, chopped

2 tablespoons extra-virgin olive oil

¼ cup coarsely chopped fresh oregano

¼ cup coarsely chopped fresh basil

zest of ½ lemon, finely chopped

sea salt and pepper

1 tablespoon fresh lemon juice

1 Cut each cherry tomato in half and add to a large salad bowl. Cut the feta cheese into large cubes and add to the tomatoes, then add the green onions.

2 Top the tomatoes and cheese with olive oil and gently toss to combine. Sprinkle salad with the herbs and lemon zest, and season to taste.

3 Just before serving, squeeze over the lemon juice.

Tomato SALAD

PREPARATION 5 mins

4 plum tomatoes, cut into wedges

6 oz/170g cherry tomatoes, halved

3 tomatoes, sliced

1 red onion, chopped

2 tablespoons red wine vinegar

¼ cup chopped fresh basil

freshly ground black pepper and sea salt

3 oz/90g assorted lettuce leaves

1 Place all the tomatoes, together with the onion, vinegar, basil, pepper and salt in a bowl and toss to combine. Set aside for 30 minutes.

2 Line a large serving platter with lettuce leaves and top with tomato mixture.

This salad can be made using any combination of tomatoes, so check the market and use what is in season and available. Heirloom tomatoes will give excellent flavor.

Greek **SALAD**

serves 4

PREPARATION 10 mins

2 Lebanese cucumbers, sliced

4 plum tomatoes, quartered

2 red onions, quartered

2½ oz/75g feta cheese, crumbled

½ cup Kalamata olives, left whole

3 tablespoons extra-virgin olive oil

2 tablespoons brown vinegar

sea salt

freshly ground black pepper

¼ cup oregano leaves

1 Place the cucumber, tomatoes, onion, cheese and olives in a bowl.

2 Combine olive oil and vinegar in a separate bowl, and whisk. Pour over the salad, then season with salt and pepper.

3 Garnish with oregano leaves. Serve salad on its own, or with fresh bread.

Herb RICE SALAD

serves 4

PREPARATION 15 mins
COOKING 10 mins

2 cups brown rice

2 oz/60g feta cheese

1½ oz/45g baby spinach

3½ oz/100g green-leaf lettuce

2 large tomatoes, deseeded and coarsely chopped

1 cucumber, deseeded and chopped

1 medium sweet yellow onion, finely chopped

1 avocado, chopped

10 large Kalamata olives, pitted and coarsely chopped

1 tablespoon chopped fresh mint

3 tablespoons chopped fresh oregano

1 cup arugula

sea salt and pepper

1½ tablespoons extra-virgin olive oil

2 tablespoons fresh lemon juice

1 Place the rice in a medium-size pot with 4 cups of water and bring to the boil. Turn down to a simmer and cook for 10 minutes or until cooked through, drain and set aside to cool.

2 Crumble the feta into a large salad bowl and add all other ingredients except the rice and the lemon juice. Gently toss to combine.

3 Pour the lemon juice over the rice and add to the rest of the salad.

4 Gently toss the salad again and serve.

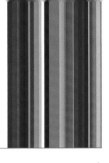

Spicy **WILD RICE SALAD**

serves 4

PREPARATION 15 mins
COOKING 25 mins

14 oz/400g wild rice blend
(brown and wild rice mix)

2 tablespoons extra-virgin
olive oil

2 onions, cut into thin wedges

1 teaspoon ground cumin

1 teaspoon ground turmeric

½ teaspoon ground cinnamon

¼ teaspoon ground cloves

¼ teaspoon ground ginger

2 carrots, thinly sliced

1 teaspoon honey

2 oranges, peeled and
segmented

3 oz/90g pistachios, toasted
and roughly chopped

3 oz/90g raisins

2 oz/60g flaked almonds,
toasted

3 spring onions, sliced

3 tablespoons chopped
fresh dill

DRESSING

1 teaspoon Dijon mustard

½ cup extra-virgin olive oil

¼ cup orange juice

1 tablespoon red wine
vinegar

1 Cook rice according to instructions on packet. Drain well and set aside to cool.

2 Heat oil in a non-stick skillet over a medium heat, add onions, cumin, turmeric, cinnamon, cloves and ginger and cook, stirring, for 10 minutes or until onions are soft and slightly caramelized. Add carrots and cook until tender. Stir in honey, then remove from heat and cool slightly.

3 Place rice, carrot mixture, oranges, pistachios, raisins, almonds, spring onions and dill in a bowl and toss to combine.

4 To make dressing, place mustard, oil, orange juice and vinegar in a bowl and whisk to combine. Pour dressing over salad and toss.

If wild rice blend is unavailable, use ¾ cup brown rice and ¼ cup wild rice. The two varieties of rice can be cooked together.

GREEN BEAN AND *Feta* SALAD

serves 4

PREPARATION **8 mins**
COOKING **8 mins**

1 lb/500g green beans, trimmed

1 sweet onion, chopped

1 teaspoon extra-virgin olive oil

8 oz/225g feta cheese

l large tomato, deseeded and chopped

¼ cup balsamic vinegar

2 tablespoons fresh lemon juice

sea salt and pepper

1 teaspoon fresh oregano leaves

1 Blanch green beans in boiling water for approximately 3–4 minutes until tender and crisp. Refresh under cold running water, then cut into bite-size pieces.

2 Sauté onion in the olive oil until tender. In a serving bowl, break feta into chunks, then mix in onion, green beans and tomato.

3 Mix balsamic and lemon juice. Pour over salad and toss well. Season to taste. Garnish with oregano leaves.

BULGUR SALAD WITH *Grilled* PEPPERS

serves 4

PREPARATION 35 mins
COOKING 20 mins

9 oz/250g bulgur wheat

2 yellow peppers, deseeded and quartered

9 oz/250g green beans, halved

2 ripe tomatoes

4 spring onions, sliced

3 oz/90g walnuts or almonds, roughly chopped

4 tablespoons chopped fresh parsley

sea salt and freshly ground black pepper

DRESSING

4 tablespoons extra-virgin olive oil

1 tablespoon wholegrain mustard

1 clove garlic, crushed

1 teaspoon balsamic vinegar

1 teaspoon white wine vinegar

1 Place the bulgur in a bowl and cover with boiling water to about 1 in/25mm above the level of the bulgur. Leave to soak for 20 minutes.

2 Meanwhile, preheat the grill to high. Grill the peppers, skin-side up, for 15–20 minutes, until the skin is blistered and blackened all over. Transfer to a plastic bag, seal and leave to cool. When cold enough to handle, remove and peel the charred skins and roughly chop the flesh.

3 Blanch the beans in boiling water for 3–4 minutes, drain, refresh under cold running water and set aside. Put the tomatoes into a bowl, cover with boiling water and leave for 30 seconds. Peel, deseed, then roughly chop the flesh.

3 Combine the ingredients for the dressing and mix well. Drain the bulgur and transfer to a salad bowl. Add the dressing and toss well. Add the vegetables, spring onions, nuts, parsley and seasoning and toss together gently to mix.

BEET AND *Bulgur* SALAD

serves 4

PREPARATION 15 mins

COOKING 30 mins

1 cup bulgur wheat

1 cup boiling water

sea salt and pepper

juice of ½ lemon

zest of 1 orange, finely grated

2 tablespoons chopped
   fresh parsley

1 teaspoon chopped fresh
   thyme

3 tablespoons extra-virgin
   olive oil

1 teaspoon Dijon mustard

¼ cup walnuts, finely chopped

1 clove garlic, crushed

2 cups boiled beets,
   coarsely chopped

1 red onion, finely chopped

1½ oz/45g Parmesan cheese,
   freshly grated

1 Combine bulgur wheat and boiling
water in a bowl. Cover and let stand for
30 minutes. Season with salt and pepper.

2 Put lemon juice, orange zest, parsley,
thyme, olive oil, mustard, walnuts and
garlic in a large bowl. Stir with a whisk
until blended.

3 Add beets, onion, bulgur wheat and
cheese to the dressing. Toss well and serve.

Main Courses

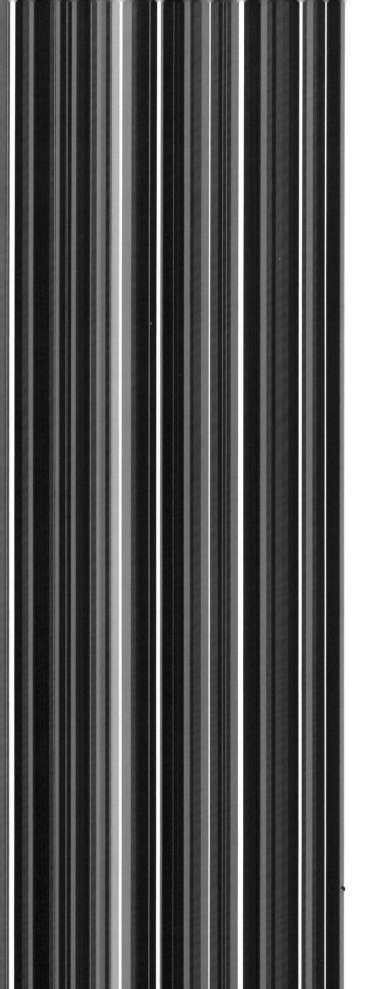

MAIN COURSES

CHICKEN BREASTS WITH FRUIT *Salsa*

serves 4

PREPARATION 25 mins
COOKING 30 mins

CHICKEN

4 skinless organic free-range chicken breast fillets

juice of ½ lemon

zest of ½ lemon

juice of ½ orange

zest of ½ orange

1 tablespoon chopped fresh mint

2 tablespoons chopped fresh cilantro

1 clove garlic, crushed

2 tablespoons extra-virgin olive oil

SALSA

1 medium mango, cubed

¼ cup chopped fresh cilantro

3 green onions, chopped

½ cup chopped pineapple

1 small red pepper, chopped

1 small tomato, deseeded and chopped

1 teaspoon extra-virgin olive oil

1 clove garlic, crushed

sea salt and pepper

1 teaspoon honey

juice of ½ lemon

1 jalapeño chili, deseeded and finely chopped

1 Combine all the chicken ingredients in a ziplock bag. Refrigerate for a few hours, up to 24 hours.

2 Put a little olive oil in a saucepan. Heat on stovetop until sizzling. Pour contents of ziplock bag, including chicken, into saucepan. Cook on stovetop until chicken is seared. Remove from heat.

3 Place in an oven at 375°F/190°C and cook until chicken is done, approximately 20 minutes. Cool for 5 minutes.

4 Meanwhile, mix all salsa ingredients together. Chill until chicken is ready.

5 Serve chicken with salsa spooned on top. Accompany with wholewheat couscous.

GRILLED *Tenderloins* WITH SPICED PUMPKIN

serves 4

PREPARATION	**40** mins
COOKING	**20** mins

18 oz/500g organic free-range chicken tenderloins

juice of 2 lemons

1 clove garlic, crushed

2 teaspoons extra-virgin olive oil

9 oz/250g potatoes, peeled, cut and rinsed

2 lb/1kg pumpkin, cut and peeled

2 tablespoons plain yogurt

1 teaspoon nutmeg

1 teaspoon allspice

1 tablespoon chopped cilantro or parsley

olive oil spray

1 medium onion, thinly sliced

2 medium tomatoes, sliced

1 Place the tenderloins in a non-metallic dish. Add the lemon juice, garlic and oil. Cover, place in the refrigerator and marinate for 40 minutes.

2 Meanwhile, boil the potatoes and pumpkin until tender, drain, and mash. Add the yogurt, nutmeg, allspice and cilantro or parsley. Set aside and keep hot.

3 Heat grill to high, spray lightly with olive oil spray and add the tenderloins, onion, and tomatoes. Cook the tenderloins for 2 minutes each side, turn the tomatoes and onion and cook until soft.

4 Pile the spiced pumpkin onto 4 heated plates, arrange the grilled tenderloins over the pumpkin and top with grilled tomato and onion.

Stuffed **CHICKEN BREAST**

serves 4

| PREPARATION | 15 mins |
| COOKING | 30 mins |

4 skinless organic free-range chicken breast fillets

sea salt and pepper

2 oz/60g fresh spinach, chopped

½ cup walnuts, finely chopped

1 tablespoon finely chopped fresh mint

½ teaspoon finely chopped fresh sage

½ teaspoon ground cinnamon

½ cup sun-dried tomatoes, coarsely chopped

zest of 1 lemon

1½ oz/45g feta cheese, crumbled

1 tablespoon extra-virgin olive oil

1 Preheat the oven to 450°F/230°C. Pound chicken breasts until they are an even thickness. Season with salt and pepper.

2 Steam the spinach until wilted. Drain excess water by squeezing spinach, then chop. Mix all remaining ingredients except olive oil in a bowl.

3 Place approximately 1 tablespoon of the spinach mixture in the center of each breast (or more, depending on the size of the chicken breast). Roll up into a cylinder.

4 Place chicken rolls in an ovenproof dish. Drizzle with olive oil, season with more salt and pepper. Place aluminum foil over the chicken and bake for approximately 15–20 minutes. Remove the foil and cook for another 5 minutes or until golden brown. Serve with wholewheat couscous or brown rice and a salad.

CHICKEN PITAS WITH *Eggplant* PURÉE

serves 4

PREPARATION 15 mins
COOKING 40 mins

4 skinless organic free-range chicken breast fillets

½ teaspoon paprika

sea salt and freshly ground black pepper

2 large eggplants

2 large garlic cloves, minced

5 teaspoons lemon juice

5 tablespoons tahini

¼ cup finely chopped fresh parsley

¼ cup finely chopped fresh mint

1 cup Greek yogurt

2 tablespoons extra-virgin olive oil

4 wholewheat pitas

1 Cut chicken breasts into cubes. Season with paprika, salt and pepper, cover and set aside in the refrigerator.

2 Char whole eggplants directly over gas flame or in broiler until skin is charred on all sides and flesh is very tender, approximately 20–30 minutes. Cool. Cut in half and spoon out pulp. Discard skins.

3 Place eggplant in a bowl and add garlic, sea salt, lemon juice, tahini, parsley and mint. Whisk until well combined and smooth. Alternatively, blend the ingredients in a food processor. Mix in the yogurt and set aside.

4 Heat the olive oil in a skillet. Add chicken, brown over a high heat, then reduce the heat and cook until tender. Remove from heat.

5 Serve chicken pieces in warmed wholewheat pita and drizzle with eggplant purée.

CHICKEN STIR-FRY WITH *Lemon* AND MANGO

serves 4

PREPARATION 18 mins
COOKING 10 mins

4 skinless organic free-range chicken breast fillets

1 ripe mango

2 tablespoons peanut oil

2 cloves garlic, crushed

1 in/25mm piece fresh ginger, finely chopped

5 oz/150g snow peas, halved lengthwise

2 sticks celery, thinly sliced

1 yellow pepper, cut into matchsticks

4 spring onions, thinly sliced

sea salt and freshly ground black pepper

juice of ½ lemon

2 tablespoons white wine or apple juice

1 tablespoon balsamic vinegar

1 tablespoon honey

2 tablespoons chopped fresh cilantro

1 Cut the chicken breasts into strips. Slice the mango flesh from either side of the stone. Cut a crisscross pattern across the flesh of each piece to separate it into small cubes, then push the skin upwards and slice off the cubes. Set aside.

2 Heat the oil in a wok or large skillet until hot. Add the garlic, ginger and chicken and stir-fry for 3 minutes.

3 Add the snow peas, celery and pepper and stir-fry for 3–4 minutes. Add the spring onions, mango and seasoning, then stir-fry for a further 2 minutes.

4 Combine the lemon juice with the wine or juice, vinegar and honey in a small bowl. Add to the chicken and vegetables and continue to cook for 2 minutes. Add the cilantro and serve immediately.

CHICKEN BREAST WITH *olives* AND RED PEPPERS

serves 4

PREPARATION 15 mins
COOKING 1 hr 10 mins

4 organic free-range chicken breast fillets

2 tablespoons extra-virgin olive oil

2 onions, finely chopped

4 red peppers, cut into large pieces

1 cup Greek olives, pitted and coarsely chopped

10 shiitake mushrooms

1 cup red wine

3 large tomatoes, diced

1 teaspoon finely chopped fresh thyme

1 teaspoon finely chopped fresh rosemary

sea salt and pepper

½ cup chicken bouillon

1 Remove the skin and trim any fat from the chicken. In a large saucepan, heat the olive oil and add the chicken. Cook for about 10 minutes until brown. Add the onion, pepper, olives and mushrooms, and sauté.

2 Add the wine, tomatoes, thyme, rosemary, salt and pepper and chicken bouillon. Bring to a simmer and cook slowly for approximately 1 hour or until chicken is cooked to your liking.

Serve with a bowl of mashed potatoes in winter or with a fresh garden salad in the summer.

COD WITH *Macadamia* NUTS
AND MANGO BASIL SAUCE

serves 4

PREPARATION 10 mins
COOKING 30 mins

4 cod fillets

sea salt and ground pepper

1½ cups chopped macadamia nuts

1 tablespoon extra-virgin olive oil

MANGO BASIL SAUCE

1½ large ripe mangoes, peeled and coarsely chopped

1 tablespoon freshly grated ginger

1½ cups vegetable or chicken bouillon

juice of ½ lime

sea salt

¼ cup fresh basil leaves

1 Season fish with salt and pepper and press into macadamia nuts to coat well.

2 Preheat oven to 400°F/200°C. Heat oil in a skillet. Cook fish until lightly browned on one side. Turn fish and place skillet in the oven. Bake for 4 minutes, then serve with the mango basil sauce.

MANGO BASIL SAUCE

1 Place all ingredients except basil leaves in a saucepan. Bring to a boil and then simmer until reduced by half.

2 Blend mixture in a blender until smooth. Coarsely chop and add basil leaves. Return to the stove to warm through.

CHAR-GRILLED TUNA WITH *Peach* SALSA

serves 4

| PREPARATION | 1 hr 15 mins |
| COOKING | 10 mins |

4 tuna steaks

1 tablespoon extra-virgin olive oil

sea salt

black pepper

4 lime wedges

1 tablespoon chopped fresh cilantro

SALSA

3 ripe peaches, finely chopped

4 spring onions, finely chopped

½ yellow pepper, finely chopped

juice of ½ lime

1 tablespoon chopped fresh cilantro

sea salt

black pepper

1 Preheat the grill to high.

2 Brush the tuna with the oil and season with salt and pepper. Grill for 3–5 minutes each side, until the fish is cooked and the flesh is beginning to flake.

3 Serve with lime wedges and peach salsa and garnish with fresh cilantro.

SALSA

1 Place the peaches, spring onions, pepper, lime juice, cilantro, salt and pepper in a small bowl and mix well. Cover and set aside for at least 1 hour to let the flavors mingle.

TUNA WITH ROASTED *Plum* TOMATOES

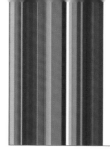

serves 4

PREPARATION	**45** mins
COOKING	**25** mins

4 tuna steaks

1 clove garlic, finely chopped

juice and zest of 1 lime

5 tablespoons extra-virgin olive oil

3 tablespoons chopped rosemary

6 plum tomatoes, halved lengthwise

1 red onion, halved and thinly sliced lengthwise

salt and black pepper

1 Put the tuna in a large dish. Mix together the garlic, lime zest, half the lime juice, 2 tablespoons of the oil, and 1 tablespoon of the rosemary and pour over the tuna. Turn to coat evenly. Cover and place in the refrigerator for 30 minutes to marinate.

2 Preheat the oven to 425°F/220°C. Place the tomatoes and onion in a shallow ovenproof dish with the remaining rosemary. Drizzle with the remaining oil and season. Roast in the oven for 15–20 minutes, until tender and lightly browned.

3 Lightly oil a ridged cast-iron grill pan or large skillet and heat over a fairly high heat. Add the tuna and cook, turning once, for 4–5 minutes or until golden.

4 Serve with the tomatoes and onion, sprinkled with the remaining lime juice.

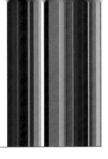

TUNA *Steaks* **WITH TOMATO SALSA**

serves 4

PREPARATION	**10** mins
COOKING	**6** mins

4 tuna steaks

2 oz/60g basil pesto

1 tablespoon extra-virgin olive oil

SALSA

2 plum tomatoes, finely chopped

1 small red onion, finely chopped

1 teaspoon coarse black pepper

sea salt

2 tablespoons chopped basil

2 tablespoons extra-virgin olive oil

juice of 1 lemon

1 Place the tuna steaks in a dish in a single layer. Combine the pesto and olive oil. Brush the fish with the pesto mixture and set aside.

2 Combine all the salsa ingredients in a small bowl, and mix well.

3 Heat a chargrill and cook the fish for 2–3 minutes on each side. Serve with salsa spooned on top.

OVEN-BAKED COD WITH
LIME AND FRESH *Herbs*

serves 4

PREPARATION **10** mins
COOKING **20** mins

4 cod steaks

juice and zest of 1 lime

juice of ½ lemon

1 tablespoon extra-virgin
   olive oil

1 teaspoon honey

1 tablespoon chopped fresh
   tarragon

1 tablespoon chopped fresh
   parsley

sea salt

black pepper

lime slices to garnish

1 Preheat the oven to 400°F/200°C.
the cod in an ovenproof dish. Place
and zest, lemon juice, oil,
ley, salt and pepper
in a s.   together until
thor   ture
ove

2 Cover the dish loosely with foil,
making sure it doesn't touch the fish.
Cook for 20 minutes, or until the fish
is tender and starting to flake.

3 Garnish with extra tarragon and
the lime slices.

Place
the lime juic
honey, tarrc
small b

COD IN *Parchment*

serves 4

PREPARATION	1 hr 15 mins
COOKING	20 mins

4 cod fillets

white pepper

4 zucchini, cut into sticks

2 carrots, cut into sticks

2 cloves garlic, minced

3 teaspoons extra-virgin
olive oil

½ cup green olives, pitted
and chopped

salt and freshly ground
pepper

¼ cup chopped fresh cilantro

½ avocado, cut into slices

TOMATO SALSA

4 ripe tomatoes, chopped

3 tablespoons finely chopped
onion

2 green chilies, deseeded and
finely chopped

½ cup chopped fresh parsley

juice of ½ lime

3 tablespoons extra-virgin
olive oil

1 Lightly season the cod with white pepper and set aside in the refrigerator. To make the salsa, mix all the ingredients together and allow to stand for one hour for the flavors to blend.

2 Preheat the oven to 400°F/200°C. Combine the zucchini, carrots, garlic, oil and olives in a bowl, add the tomato salsa and season with salt and pepper.

3 Lay out four pieces of baking paper and divide half of the vegetable mixture between them, top each with a cod fillet and top again with remaining vegetable mixture.

4 Fold the paper, making sure the sides are well tucked in. Bake in the oven for 20 minutes. Serve with fresh cilantro and avocado slices.

SIMPLY *Seasoned* COD FILLETS

serves 4

PREPARATION	5 mins
COOKING	10 mins

2 tablespoons wholewheat pastry flour

sea salt and black pepper

4 cod fillets

2 tablespoons extra-virgin olive oil

1 tablespoon chopped fresh parsley

lemon wedges

1 Put the flour onto a large plate and season with salt and pepper. Dip both sides of the fish fillets into the seasoned flour and gently shake to remove any excess. Place the floured fillets on a clean plate.

2 Put half the oil into a large skillet over a medium heat. When hot, add two of the fillets. If the fillets still have skins, add them skin-side up.

3 Fry the fillets for 3–4 minutes, until the undersides are golden, then turn them over. Fry for another 3–4 minutes, until c through. Transfer the fillets to g and wrap loosely to ke

4 Wipe the skillet clean, then add the remaining oil and heat. Cook the remaining two fillets as above.

5 Transfer the fish to plates, sprinkle with parsley and serve with lemon wedges.

To check if fish is cooked, remove a small flake from the thickest part – it should be soft and completely opaque, not translucent.

FISH STEW WITH *Lemongrass* AND COCONUT MILK

serves 4

PREPARATION 20 mins
COOKING 30 mins

2 tablespoons extra-virgin olive oil

2 green chilies, deseeded and sliced

2 stalks lemongrass, bruised and sliced lengthwise

4 cloves garlic, thinly sliced

2 carrots, thinly sliced

2 small sweet potatoes, thinly sliced

½ small head of broccoli, cut into florets

1 cup fish bouillon

14 fl oz/400mL coconut milk

9 oz/250g monkfish, cut into bite-size pieces

12 oz/340g raw peeled tiger prawns

1 bunch spring onions, shredded

6 oz/170g scallops

juice and zest of 1 lime

1 tablespoon chopped fresh chives

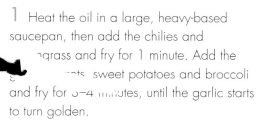

1 Heat the oil in a large, heavy-based saucepan, then add the chilies and ___ngrass and fry for 1 minute. Add the ___ sweet potatoes and broccoli and fry for 3–4 minutes, until the garlic starts to turn golden.

2 Stir in the bouillon and coconut milk and bring to the boil, then reduce the heat and simmer, uncovered, for 15 minutes or until reduced slightly.

3 Add the monkfish to the coconut milk mixture, then cover and simmer for 4–5 minutes, until the fish has started to turn opaque. Meanwhile, slit open the back of each prawn and devein with a small knife. Add the spring onions, scallops and prawns to the stew and cook for 3–4 minutes, until the prawns have turned pink and the scallops are tender and cooked through. Stir in the lime juice and zest, and remove the lemongrass. Serve garnished with chopped chives.

You can substitute salmon or cod for the monkfish.

Soy-Glazed FISH

serves 4

PREPARATION 1 hr
COOKING 5 mins

1½ lbs/750g firm white fish, such as cod or halibut

1 tablespoon sesame oil

3 green onions, chopped

MARINADE

2 tablespoons tamari

2 tablespoons sesame oil

2 tablespoons dry sherry

1 clove garlic, minced

½ cup spring onions, chopped

3 tablespoons fresh minced ginger

SAUCE

2 tablespoons honey

3 tablespoons tamari

2 tablespoons sesame oil

2 tablespoons sesame seeds

2 tablespoons dry sherry

2 star anise

1 cinnamon stick

1 Place fish and marinade ingredients in a ziplock bag. Refrigerate for one hour.

2 Meanwhile, place all sauce ingredients in a small saucepan. Bring to a boil, stirring constantly. Reduce heat and simmer, uncovered, until sauce thickens, approximately 5 minutes. Remove star anise and cinnamon stick, and cool.

3 Remove fish from marinade. Heat the sesame oil in a hot skillet, then add the fish. Cook approximately 1–2 minutes before turning, then cook for another minute.

4 Add marinade to fish and cook for another minute. When fish is opaque and becoming firm, remove from skillet.

5 Serve drizzled with sauce and garnished with green onions.

FISH BAKED IN CORN *Husks*

serves 4

PREPARATION **40 mins**
COOKING **12 mins**

48 dried corn husks

4 firm white fish fillets

3 tablespoons fresh cilantro

1 avocado, sliced

pickled jalapeños

corn or wholewheat flour
tortillas, warmed

CHILI LIME PASTE

3 cloves garlic, chopped

2 mild fresh green chilies,
chopped

2 tablespoons fresh oregano
leaves

2 tablespoons mild chili
powder

zest of 2 limes

1 teaspoon ground cumin

¼ cup lime juice

1 Place the corn husks in a bowl, cover with warm water and soak for 30 minutes.

2 Preheat the oven to 425°F/220°C. Cut each fish fillet in half lengthwise, then spread both sides with the chili lime paste.

3 Overlap 2–3 corn husks, place a piece of fish on top, then cover with more husks. Fold to enclose the fish and tie to secure. Place the parcels on a baking tray and bake for 10–12 minutes or until the fish flakes when tested with a fork.

4 To serve, open the fish parcels, scatter with cilantro and accompany with avocado, pickled jalapeños and tortillas.

CHILI LIME PASTE

1 Place the garlic, chilies, oregano, chili powder, lime zest, cumin and lime juice in a food processor and process until smooth.

SNAPPER WITH *Wine* AND PARSLEY

serves 4

PREPARATION 10 mins
COOKING 12 mins

½ cup wholewheat pastry flour

1 teaspoon coarsely ground pepper

¼ teaspoon sea salt

4 snapper fillets

3 tablespoons extra-virgin olive oil

2 cloves garlic, crushed

½ cup white wine

2 tablespoons finely chopped parsley

1 Combine the flour, pepper and salt in a dish, and coat the fish fillets evenly with the seasoned flour, shaking off any excess.

2 Heat 2 tablespoons of the oil in a skillet, add the fish, and cook over a medium heat for 5–6 minutes on each side, depending on the thickness of the fish. Set the fish aside on a plate, and keep warm.

3 Wipe the skillet clean, then add the remaining oil and the garlic, and cook for 2 minutes. Add the white wine and simmer until the sauce reduces.

4 Just before serving, add the parsley to the sauce and serve drizzled over the fish.

MIXED SEAFOOD WITH *Spicy* SAUCE

serves 4

PREPARATION 1 hr 15 mins
COOKING 10 mins

1 lb/500g shrimp

1 lb/500g salmon

6 large tomatoes, halved

1 large fennel bulb, stalks removed, cut into quarters

3 large carrots, cut in half lengthwise

1 large zucchini, cut in half lengthwise

2 large mushrooms

¼ cup extra-virgin olive oil

1 unpeeled orange, cut into 1 in/25mm slices

3 cloves garlic, crushed

SAUCE

2 large red peppers, roasted

1 teaspoon ground cilantro

1 teaspoon ground cumin

1 teaspoon ground cinnamon

1 tablespoon fresh oregano

3 tablespoons coarsely chopped fresh cilantro

1 small jalapeño, deseeded and finely chopped

juice of 1 lemon

⅓ cup extra-virgin olive oil

½ cup walnuts, chopped

zest of 1 orange

sea salt and pepper

1 avocado, coarsely chopped

1 Shell and devein the shrimp, then place with the salmon, vegetables and mushrooms in a large bowl. Mix olive oil, orange slices, and garlic, and drizzle over the fish and vegetables. Toss thoroughly to coat, cover and stand in the refrigerator for 1 hour.

2 Heat a grill and cook the marinated seafood and vegetables for 5 minutes. Coat with any remaining marinade, gently turn and cook for a further 3–4 minutes.

3 To make the sauce, place all ingredients except salt, pepper and avocado in a food processor. Pulse until mixture is almost smooth. Season and add avocado.

4 Serve seafood with sauce at the side, or top the salmon pieces with the sauce.

SUMMER *Shrimp* PASTA

serves 4

PREPARATION 15 mins
COOKING 15 mins

1 lb/500g raw shrimp

¼ cup green olives, chopped

¼ cup black olives, chopped

8 medium tomatoes, peeled and coarsely chopped

2 cloves garlic, crushed

1 tablespoon red pepper flakes

1 cup coarsely chopped basil leaves

½ cup coarsely chopped flat-leaf parsley

¼ cup capers, drained

6 tablespoons extra-virgin olive oil

¼ cup toasted pine nuts

2 anchovies, finely chopped

1 lb/500g uncooked wholewheat spaghetti

sea salt and pepper

juice and zest of 1 lemon

1 Peel and devein the shrimp, and set aside in the refrigerator. Place olives, tomatoes, garlic, red pepper flakes, basil, parsley, capers, 4 tablespoons of the oil, the pine nuts and anchovies in a large bowl. Toss well to combine.

2 Cook pasta in salted boiling water until al dente.

3 Heat the remainder of the oil in a skillet. Add the shrimp and cook on each side until pink. Season with salt and pepper. Stir in lemon juice and zest. Mix well.

4 Add shrimp and pasta to olive and tomato mixture. Toss to combine and serve.

Vegetable Dishes

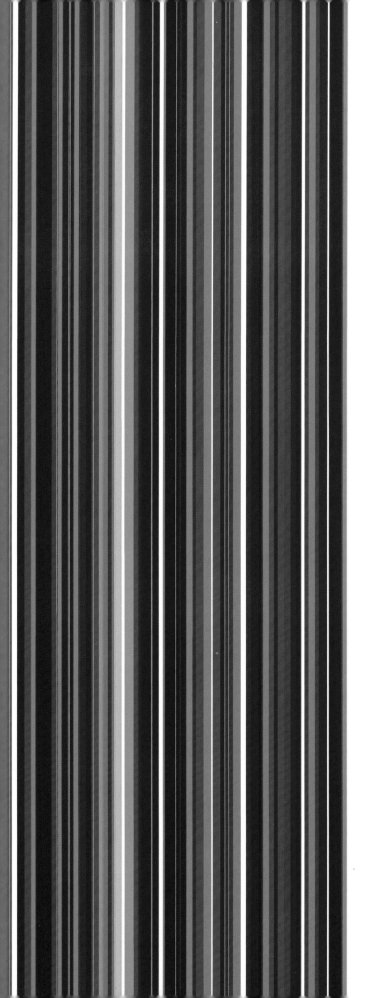

VEGETABLE DISHES

Fettuccine **WITH GRILLED VEGETABLES**

serves 4

PREPARATION 15 mins
COOKING 15 mins

2 fennel bulbs, stalks removed

16 oz/450g asparagus, trimmed

4 tablespoons extra-virgin olive oil

sea salt and freshly ground pepper

1 cup green peas

16 oz/450g wholewheat fettuccine

2 tablespoons coarsely chopped flat-leaf parsley

1 tablespoon coarsely chopped rosemary

1 tablespoon coarsely chopped mint

zest of 1 lemon

1½ oz/45g Parmesan cheese, coarsely grated

15 oz/425g canned cannellini beans, drained and rinsed

1 Cut fennel bulbs into coarse slices. Cut asparagus into 1 in/25mm pieces and combine with fennel in a bowl. Drizzle over 1 tablespoon of the oil and season with salt and pepper.

2 Grill until just tender. Return warm vegetables to bowl and add peas.

3 Cook pasta in salted boiling water according to package directions. Drain and pour into a large serving bowl.

4 Add the vegetables, the remainder of the oil, the parsley, rosemary, mint, lemon zest, cheese and cannellini beans, and season with more salt and pepper. Toss well and serve.

ROASTED VEGETABLE AND *Broccoli* COUSCOUS

serves 4

PREPARATION 20 mins
COOKING 50 mins

3 parsnips, cut into chunks

2 sweet potatoes, cut into chunks

3 turnips, quartered

2 cloves garlic, crushed

6 tablespoons extra-virgin olive oil

sea salt

5 tablespoons honey

7 oz/200g wholewheat couscous

12 oz/340g tomatoes, chopped

¼ cup chopped parsley

¼ cup chopped chives

¼ cup chopped basil

juice of 1 lemon

7 oz/200g broccoli, cut into florets

1 Preheat the oven to 400°F/200°C.

2 Cook the parsnips in boiling salted water for 2 minutes, then drain. Place in a roasting pan with the sweet potatoes, turnips, garlic and 3 tablespoons of oil, turning to coat. Sprinkle with salt, then bake for 30 minutes or until lightly browned.

3 Drizzle the honey over the vegetables, then return them to the oven for 10 minutes or until browned and glossy.

4 Meanwhile, prepare the couscous according to the packet instructions. Heat the rest of the oil in a skillet and cook the tomatoes for 2–3 minutes, until softened. Add the couscous and heat through, then mix in the herbs and lemon juice.

5 Meanwhile, steam the broccoli florets until tender. Serve the couscous with the roasted vegetables and broccoli arranged on top.

When roasted, vegetables caramelize naturally. Glazing them with honey adds extra gloss and makes them taste even sweeter.

Tofu STIR-FRY

serves 4

PREPARATION 20 mins
COOKING 10 mins

2 tablespoons extra-virgin
  olive oil

2 cloves garlic, finely
  chopped

1 in/25mm piece ginger,
  finely chopped

1 large red onion, sliced

4 sticks celery, thinly sliced

1 large red pepper,
  cut into strips

2 carrots, cut into julienne
  strips

7 oz/200g green beans,
  blanched

3½ oz/100g broccoli florets,
  blanched

4 tablespoons light soy sauce

6 tablespoons dry sherry

2 teaspoons honey

7 oz/200g snow peas

14 oz/400g firm tofu, cubed

1 Heat the oil in a wok or large skillet, add the garlic, ginger and onion and stir-fry over a high heat for 1 minute. Add the celery, pepper, carrot, beans and broccoli and stir-fry for 3 minutes.

2 Mix the soy sauce, sherry and honey together in a bowl and add to the vegetables along with the snow peas and tofu. Stir-fry for a further 2 minutes and serve immediately with steamed or boiled brown rice or soba noodles.

GREEN VEGETABLE STIR-FRY WITH *Sesame* SEEDS

PREPARATION 10 mins

COOKING 15 mins

2 tablespoons sesame seeds

2 tablespoons peanut oil

1 clove garlic, roughly chopped

1 in/25mm piece fresh ginger, finely chopped

5 oz/150g broccoli, cut into very small florets

2 zucchini, halved lengthwise and finely sliced

6 oz/170g snow peas

1 tablespoon rice wine or medium-dry sherry

1 tablespoon dark soy sauce

1 tablespoon oyster sauce

1 Heat a wok. Add the sesame seeds and dry-fry for 2 minutes or until golden, shaking the pan frequently. Remove and set aside.

2 Add the oil to the wok, heat for 1 minute, then add the garlic and ginger and stir-fry over a medium heat for 1–2 minutes, until softened. Add the broccoli and stir-fry for a further 2–3 minutes.

3 Add the zucchini and snow peas and stir-fry for 3 minutes. Pour over the rice wine or sherry and sizzle for 1 minute. Add the soy and oyster sauces, mix well, then stir-fry for 2 minutes.

4 Sprinkle over the fried sesame seeds just before serving.

Prepare all the vegetables before you start cooking – this will ensure you don't overcook what's in the wok while preparing the next ingredient.

EASY *vegetable* STIR-FRY

serves 4

PREPARATION 20 mins
COOKING 10 mins

3½ oz/100g dried
mushrooms

2 teaspoons sesame oil

2 cloves garlic, crushed

1 tablespoon grated fresh
ginger

1 large onion, sliced

1 red pepper, cut into strips

2 carrots, sliced diagonally

9 oz/250g broccoli, cut into
florets

3 stalks celery, sliced
diagonally

15 oz/425g canned baby
corn, rinsed and drained

7 oz/200g firm tofu, chopped

2 tablespoons sweet chili
sauce

2 tablespoons soy sauce

4 tablespoons cashew nuts

1 Place the mushrooms in a bowl and cover with boiling water. Set aside for 15–20 minutes or until the mushrooms are tender. Drain, remove the stalks if necessary, and slice.

2 Heat the oil in a wok, add the garlic, ginger and onion and stir-fry over a medium heat for 3 minutes or until the onion is soft.

3 Add the pepper, carrot, broccoli and celery and stir-fry for 3 minutes longer.

4 Add the mushrooms, corn, tofu, chili sauce, soy sauce and cashew nuts and stir-fry for 1 more minute. Serve immediately.

SWEET POTATO AND *Tofu* CURRY

serves 4

PREPARATION 10 mins
COOKING 30 mins

1 tablespoon extra-virgin olive oil

1 teaspoon chili oil

10 oz/280g firm tofu, cut into ½ in/1cm-thick slices

1½ cups coconut cream

1 cup vegetable bouillon

2 teaspoons Thai red curry paste

1 teaspoon turmeric

13 oz/370g sweet potato, cut into 1 in/25mm cubes

1 small carrot, finely chopped

½ cup green peas

2 teaspoons honey

1 tablespoon fish sauce

2 teaspoons lime juice

½ cup fresh basil leaves

1 Heat olive oil and chili oil in a wok or large saucepan over a medium heat, add tofu and stir-fry until brown on all sides. Remove, drain on absorbent paper and set aside.

2 Wipe wok or saucepan clean, then add coconut cream and bouillon and bring to the boil. Stir in curry paste and turmeric and cook for 3–4 minutes or until fragrant.

3 Add sweet potato, cover and cook over a medium heat for 8–10 minutes or until sweet potato is almost cooked. Add carrot and peas.

4 Stir in honey, fish sauce and lime juice and cook for 4–5 minutes longer or until sweet potato is tender. Stir in basil and serve immediately.

PEANUT *Soba* NOODLES

serves 4

PREPARATION 10 mins
COOKING 10 mins

10 oz/280g soba noodles

½ tablespoon extra-virgin
olive oil

2 cups snow peas, trimmed

2 carrots, finely sliced

7 oz/200g firm tofu,
cut into cubes

1 cup shiitake mushrooms

1 in/25mm piece fresh
ginger, finely chopped

2 cloves garlic, finely
chopped

½ cup vegetable bouillon

1 tablespoon honey

2 tablespoons tamari

¼ cup smooth peanut butter

½ cup finely chopped fresh
cilantro

1 tablespoon sesame seeds

¼ cup finely chopped peanuts

1 Cook soba noodles according to package directions. Drain and set aside.

2 Heat the oil in a skillet and stir-fry snow peas, carrots, tofu and mushrooms until they soften. Add the ginger and garlic and cook for a few minutes. Remove from heat and keep warm.

3 In a small bowl, mix bouillon, honey and tamari until well combined. Place this mixture with the peanut butter in a small saucepan and simmer on low heat until the sauce thickens, stirring well.

4 Pour this mixture over the vegetables and noodles and toss to combine. Add the cilantro, sesame seeds and chopped peanuts, and serve.

MUSHROOM AND GOAT'S CHEESE *Strudel*

serves 4

PREPARATION	25 mins
COOKING	35 mins

500g mixed mushrooms, such as shiitake, Swiss and oyster

1 teaspoon extra-virgin olive oil

2 green onions, finely diced

2 cloves garlic, crushed

½ cup white wine

1 teaspoon lemon juice

olive oil spray

3 oz/90g feta cheese, crumbled

3 tablespoons chopped fresh mixed herbs, for example, sage, thyme, oregano, rosemary

8 sheets wholewheat phyllo pastry

sea salt and freshly ground black pepper

1 Dice the mushrooms. Heat the oil in a skillet over a low heat. Add the onions and garlic. Cook, stirring, for 2–3 minutes or until soft and translucent. Add the mushrooms. Cook, stirring occasionally, for 5–8 minutes or until juices evaporate. Stir in the wine and lemon juice. Cook, stirring occasionally, until liquid is absorbed, then cool.

2 Preheat the oven to 350°F/180°C. Lightly spray or brush a baking tray with olive oil or line with non-stick baking paper. Set aside.

3 Stir the cheese and fresh herbs into the mushroom mixture. Lay 2 sheets of phyllo pastry on a clean, dry work surface. Lightly spray or brush with olive oil and season with salt and pepper. Place 2 more sheets on top. Place half the mushroom mixture along the long edge, leaving a 1 in/25mm border at each end. Fold in the ends and roll up tightly. Place strudel, seam down, on the baking tray. Repeat with remaining phyllo and mushroom mixture to make a second strudel.

4 Using a sharp knife, make slashes in the top of each strudel to mark slices. Bake for 10–12 minutes or until golden.

DHAL WITH *Ginger* AND CILANTRO

serves 4

PREPARATION 10 mins
COOKING 40 mins

7 oz/200g dried red lentils

½ teaspoon turmeric

1 tablespoon extra-virgin olive oil

½ in/1cm piece fresh ginger, finely chopped

1 teaspoon cumin seeds

1 teaspoon ground cilantro

2 carrots, peeled and finely chopped

sea salt and black pepper

4 tablespoons chopped fresh cilantro, plus extra leaves to garnish

½ teaspoon paprika

1 Rinse the lentils in cold water and drain well, then place in a large saucepan with 18 fl oz/800mL of water. Bring to the boil and skim, then stir in the turmeric. Reduce the heat and partly cover the pan. Simmer for 30–35 minutes until thickened, stirring every now and then.

2 Heat the oil in a small skillet, then add the ginger and cumin seeds and fry for 30 seconds or until the cumin seeds start to pop. Stir in the ground cilantro and fry for 1 minute. Add the carrots.

3 Season the lentils with plenty of salt and pepper, then add the toasted spices and carrots. Stir in the chopped cilantro, mixing well. Transfer to a serving dish and garnish with the paprika and extra cilantro leaves.

RED ONION, *Zucchini* AND TOMATO PIZZA

serves 4

PREPARATION 25 mins
COOKING 30 mins

1 tablespoon extra-virgin olive oil

2 small red onions, sliced

1 yellow pepper, sliced

2 small zucchini, sliced

1 clove garlic, crushed

4 tablespoons tomato purée

1 tablespoon tomato paste

1 tablespoon chopped fresh mixed herbs

sea salt

freshly ground black pepper

3 small plum tomatoes, sliced

1 oz/30g Parmesan cheese, grated

1 oz/30g mozzarella cheese, grated

¼ cup fresh basil

PIZZA DOUGH

2 cups wholegrain flour

2 teaspoons baking powder

½ oz/15g non-hydrogenated margarine substitute, such as Earth Balance

½ cup low-fat milk

1 tablespoon water

1 Preheat the oven to 425°F/220°C.

2 Heat the oil in a saucepan, then add the onion, pepper, zucchini and garlic and cook for 5 minutes or until softened, stirring occasionally. Set aside.

3 To make the pizza dough, place the flour and baking powder in a bowl, then rub in the margarine substitute with your fingers. Stir in the milk to form a smooth dough, add the water and knead lightly. Rest the dough for 15 minutes.

4 Roll the dough out on a lightly floured surface to a circle about 16 in/40cm wide, then transfer to an oiled sheet of baking paper. Mix together the tomato purée, tomato paste, mixed herbs, salt and pepper and spread over the dough. Top with the onion mixture.

5 Arrange the tomato slices on top and sprinkle with the Parmesan and mozzarella. Bake for 25–30 minutes, until the cheese is golden brown and bubbling. Garnish with fresh basil.

WHOLEWHEAT *Burrito*

serves 4

PREPARATION **10 mins**
COOKING **20 mins**

4 wholewheat tortillas

1½ oz/45g low-fat or
   soy cheese, shredded

14 oz/400g black beans,
   drained and rinsed

½ cup corn kernels

3 tomatoes, coarsely chopped

¼ cup chopped spring onions

2 cups green-leaf lettuce,
   coarsely chopped

1 bunch coarsely chopped
   cilantro

½ cup Greek yogurt

¾ cup tomato salsa
   (see page 106)

1 Preheat the oven to 325°F/160°C. Lay a tortilla on a plate, then spoon on cheese and 2–3 tablespoons of black beans, place in oven until cheese starts to melt.

2 Remove from the oven and add corn, tomatoes, spring onions, lettuce, cilantro, yogurt and salsa. Carefully roll tortilla, folding in the edges. Repeat with the remaining tortillas.

3 Garnish with additional salsa and a dollop of yogurt. Serve immediately.

Try making these burritos with different fillings, for example, 14 oz/400g drained and rinsed pinto beans, 2 coarsely chopped avocados, 1 chopped red pepper, or ½ cup brown rice.

MUSHROOM *Feta* PARCELS

makes 24

PREPARATION 15 mins

COOKING 25 mins

1 small onion, finely chopped

2 tablespoons extra-virgin
olive oil

1lb/500g chopped fresh
mushrooms, for example,
shiitake, porcini and white

1 teaspoon chopped fresh
oregano

¼ teaspoon crushed fresh
rosemary leaves

1 teaspoon chopped fresh
parsley

2 tablespoons pesto

3½ oz/100g feta cheese,
crumbled

sea salt and pepper to taste

13 oz/370g wholewheat
phyllo pastry sheets

1 Preheat the oven to 400°F/200°C.

2 Sauté onion in 1 tablespoon of the olive oil until translucent. Add mushrooms and cook until soft. Add oregano, rosemary, parsley and pesto. Stir, then add feta and season to taste.

3 Brush 2–3 stacked sheets of phyllo with olive oil. Cut into circles approximately 4 in/10cm in diameter – use a scone cutter or cup. Spoon a tablespoon of the mushroom filling into the center of each pastry disk. Gather the sides of each pastry together and gently twist the top.

4 Brush the outside of the pastry with a little olive oil. Place the mushroom parcels on an oiled baking sheet and bake until golden brown, approximately 12 minutes.

Stuffed TOMATOES WITH GARBANZO BEANS AND CILANTRO

serves 4

PREPARATION 20 mins

COOKING 50 mins

2 slices stale wholewheat bread

4 large tomatoes

1 clove garlic, crushed

½ cup canned garbanzo beans, rinsed

juice of 1 lemon

1 tablespoon extra-virgin olive oil

1 red onion, finely chopped

¼ teaspoon cayenne pepper

1 teaspoon turmeric

1 teaspoon ground cumin

1 teaspoon ground cilantro

4 tablespoons chopped fresh cilantro

sea salt and black pepper

1 Preheat the oven to 325°F/160°C.

2 Place bread in oven for 20 minutes or until it becomes crisp. Process in a food processor to make breadcrumbs. Increase the oven temperature to 400°F/200°C.

3 Slice off the tomato tops and scoop out the insides. Place the shells upside down on absorbent paper to drain. Put the insides and tops into a food processor with the garlic, garbanzo beans and lemon juice and blend to a purée.

4 Heat the oil, then cook the onion with the cayenne pepper, turmeric, cumin and ground cilantro for 4–5 minutes, until softened. Mix with the tomato mixture, breadcrumbs, fresh cilantro and seasoning.

5 Spoon the mixture into the tomato shells. Place them on a lightly oiled baking sheet and bake for 25 minutes or until tender.

TUSCAN VEGETABLE *Terrine*

serves 4

PREPARATION 30 mins
COOKING 30 mins

300g pumpkin or butternut squash, peeled

extra-virgin olive oil for brushing

16 plum tomatoes

14 oz/400g fresh mozzarella cheese

1 bunch fresh basil

sea salt and freshly ground black pepper

1 bunch arugula

MUSTARD AND BALSAMIC DRESSING

1 teaspoon wholegrain mustard

2 tablespoons balsamic vinegar

2 tablespoons extra-virgin olive oil

1 Preheat the oven to 350°F/180°C. Line a terrine or loaf dish with plastic wrap, leaving enough overhanging the sides to cover top of terrine. Set aside.

2 Cut pumpkin or squash into ½ in/1cm-thick slices to fit shape of terrine – there should be enough for a single layer.

3 Lightly brush slices with olive oil. Place on a baking tray. Bake for 20–30 minutes or until pumpkin or squash is cooked but still firm. Cool.

4 Cut tomatoes in half lengthwise. Remove seeds and press gently with hands to flatten. Cut cheese into ¼ in/5mm-thick slices.

5 Layer ingredients in the terrine in the following order: tomatoes, basil leaves, cheese, tomatoes, pumpkin or squash, cheese, basil leaves, tomatoes and finally cheese. The overall effect should be layers of tomatoes, basil and cheese with a layer of pumpkin or squash in the centre. When layering, place the tomatoes skin-side down and season each tomato layer with a little sea salt and black pepper.

6 Cover terrine with the overhanging plastic wrap. Weigh down with a plate and refrigerate overnight.

7 To make the dressing, place mustard, vinegar and oil in a screw-top jar. Shake well to combine.

8 To serve, carefully lift terrine from dish, using the plastic wrap. Cut into thick slices. Line serving plates with arugula leaves. Place a slice of terrine on top and drizzle with dressing. Serve with Italian bread.

MIXED VEGETABLES IN *Tomato* SAUCE

serves 4

PREPARATION 15 mins
COOKING 1 hr

1½ lb/750g Yukon gold potatoes

1½ lb/750g sweet potatoes

3 zucchini

3 carrots

2 medium eggplants

1 red pepper

1 yellow pepper

1 green pepper

1 fennel bulb

3 sweet onions

4 tomatoes, thickly sliced

4 large cloves garlic, sliced

¼ cup extra-virgin olive oil

sea salt and pepper

2 tablespoons finely chopped mint

2 tablespoons chopped flat-leaf parsley

1 oz/30g feta cheese, crumbled

1 Preheat oven to 325°F/160°C. Slice vegetables into similar sizes, except for the potatoes, which should be half the thickness of the other vegetables.

2 Place vegetables in a large ovenproof dish. Add tomatoes, garlic, olive oil, salt, pepper and 1 tablespoon each of the mint and parsley, toss well.

3 Bake for approximately 1 hour until tender. Remove from heat. Add the remaining mint and parsley and the feta, toss and serve.

Side Dishes

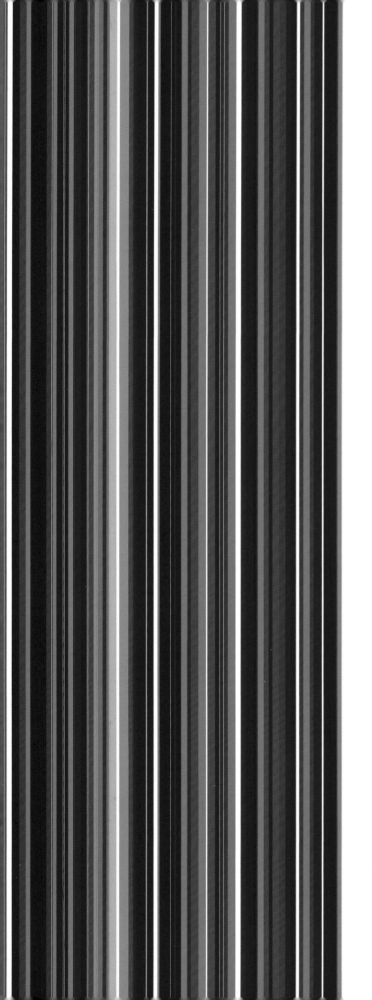

SIDE DISHES

Lemon-Roasted VEGETABLES

serves 4

PREPARATION 15 mins
COOKING 1 hr

2 potatoes, thinly sliced

1 large sweet onion,
thinly sliced

1 tablespoon coarse sea salt

¼ cup extra-virgin olive oil

2 carrots, sliced

4 large sprigs fresh rosemary

100g Brussels sprouts,
quartered

50g mushrooms, coarsely
chopped

2 lemons, thickly sliced

2 tablespoons coarsely
chopped fresh basil

HERB DRESSING

1 tablespoon extra-virgin
olive oil

1 clove garlic, crushed

½ tablespoon fresh lemon
juice

¼ teaspoon sea salt

1 tablespoon chopped
fresh oregano

1 tablespoon chopped
fresh basil

1 Preheat oven to 400°F/200°C.
To make the herb dressing, combine all
ingredients in a screw-top jar and shake
well to combine.

2 In an ovenproof baking dish, place
potatoes and onion, 1 teaspoon of the salt
and the herb dressing. Toss, then cover
lightly with foil and bake for 30 minutes.

3 Remove from oven and add olive oil,
carrots, rosemary and Brussels sprouts,
toss to combine. Bake for approximately
15 minutes. Remove from heat and add
mushrooms, lemon slices and remaining
salt, toss to combine.

4 Cover and return to oven for
approximately 15 minutes.

5 Remove from oven and add basil.
Remove lemons and rosemary sprigs.
Drizzle with a little extra olive oil and
lemon juice and serve.

Harvest VEGETABLE BAKE

serves 4

| PREPARATION | 10 mins |
| COOKING | 1 hr 30 mins |

1 onion, sliced

2 leeks, sliced

2 sticks celery, chopped

2 carrots, thinly sliced

1 red pepper, sliced

1 lb/500g mixed root vegetables, such as sweet potato and parsnip, cubed

1 small butternut squash, peeled and cubed

3 oz/90g mushrooms, sliced

14 oz/400g canned chopped tomatoes

6 tablespoons dry cider

1 tablespoon chopped fresh thyme

1 tablespoon chopped fresh oregano

freshly ground black pepper

sea salt

1 Preheat the oven to 350°F/180°C. Place the onion, leeks, celery, carrots, pepper, root vegetables, butternut squash and mushrooms in a large, ovenproof casserole dish and mix well. Stir in the tomatoes, cider, thyme, oregano, black pepper and sea salt.

2 Cover and bake in the center of the oven for 1–1½ hours, until the vegetables are cooked through and tender, stirring once or twice. Garnish with fresh basil and serve with warm crusty wholewheat bread.

This dish is especially good in autumn, when the ingredients are in season.

INDIAN-STYLE *Spinach*

serves 4

PREPARATION	15 mins
COOKING	5 mins

2 tablespoons extra-virgin olive oil

4 large shallots, thinly sliced

2 large cloves garlic, thinly sliced

2 in/5cm piece fresh ginger, finely chopped

2 teaspoons ground cumin

2 teaspoons ground turmeric

2 lb/1kg fresh spinach, stems removed, well drained

2 teaspoons whole yellow mustard seeds

sea salt and freshly ground pepper

2 tablespoons raisins

1 Heat oil in skillet. Add shallots and garlic, and brown. Stir in ginger, cumin and turmeric, and cook for 1 minute.

2 Add spinach and mustard seeds. Season with salt and pepper. Toss until spinach starts to wilt.

3 Remove from skillet. Add raisins and serve immediately.

Asian GREEN BEAN STIR-FRY

serves 4

PREPARATION 5 mins

COOKING 10 mins

1 teaspoon sesame oil

500g baby green beans

2 teaspoons light soy sauce

2 teaspoons toasted sesame
seeds

2 tablespoons toasted flaked
almonds

1 thinly sliced spring onion

1 Heat a wok and pour in the oil. Add the
beans and stir-fry for 1–2 minutes.

2 Add the soy sauce, sesame seeds,
almonds and spring onion, and stir-fry
for a further minute. Serve immediately.

You can also use fresh young asparagus when it's in season, instead of the beans.

BAKED *French* FRIES

serves 4

PREPARATION	**10 mins**
COOKING	**35 mins**

3 large baking potatoes, skin on, sliced into thick French fries

2 large sweet potatoes, skin on, sliced into thick French fries

1½ tablespoons extra-virgin olive oil

coarse salt and freshly ground black pepper

3 sprigs fresh rosemary, finely chopped

1 Preheat oven to 425°F/220°C. Toss all ingredients in a large bowl.

2 Place on a baking sheet and bake for 15 minutes. Using a spatula, turn the fries over and return quickly to the oven. Cook for another 15 minutes, then turn the fries again. Bake for 5 minutes longer or until golden and crisp.

ZUCCHINI, BEAN AND TOMATO *Medley*

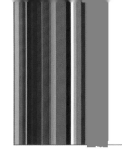

serves 4

| PREPARATION 15 mins |
| COOKING 20 mins |

2 tablespoons extra-virgin olive oil

1 large onion, sliced

1 clove garlic, crushed

1 teaspoon chopped fresh thyme or oregano

pinch of sea salt

freshly ground black pepper

1 lb/500g green beans, cut into short lengths

1 lb/500g zucchini, cut into chunks

4 large tomatoes, quartered

¼ cup water

toasted sliced almonds or toasted pine nuts

1 Heat the oil in a large, heavy-based skillet over moderate heat and cook the onion and garlic, stirring, for 5–8 minutes or until the onion is golden. Stir in the thyme or oregano and season to taste with salt and pepper.

2 Add the green beans, zucchini, tomatoes and water to the pan, mix lightly, cover and simmer gently for 10 minutes or until the vegetables are just tender.

3 Garnish with toasted almonds or pine nuts and serve.

SPINACH WITH *Sesame* SEEDS

serves 4

PREPARATION 18 mins

COOKING 10 mins

25 oz/700g fresh spinach

1 tablespoon peanut oil

1 teaspoon sesame oil

3 cloves garlic, chopped

2 tablespoons sesame seeds

juice of ½ lemon

¼ teaspoon finely grated
   lemon zest

sea salt and black pepper

1 Remove the stalks from the spinach, then place in a large bowl, cover with boiling water and leave for 2–3 minutes. Drain, then refresh under cold running water. Squeeze out any excess water, then coarsely chop.

2 Heat the peanut and sesame oils in a wok or large heavy-based skillet. Add the garlic and sesame seeds and stir-fry for 1–2 minutes, until the garlic begins to brown and the seeds start to pop.

3 Stir in the spinach and stir-fry for 1–2 minutes, until heated through. Add the lemon juice and zest, season and mix well, then serve.

SNOW PEAS AND *Carrots* WITH SESAME SEEDS

serves 4

PREPARATION 10 mins

COOKING 5 mins

½ cucumber

2 tablespoons sesame seeds

1 tablespoon peanut oil

4 carrots, cut into matchsticks

9 oz/250g snow peas

6 spring onions, chopped

1 tablespoon lemon juice

sea salt

black pepper

1 Peel the cucumber, cut in half lengthwise and scoop out the seeds. Thinly slice into half moons.

2 Heat a non-stick wok or large skillet. Add the sesame seeds and dry-fry for 1 minute or until toasted, tossing constantly. Remove and set aside. Add the oil, then the cucumber and carrots and stir-fry over a high heat for 2 minutes. Add the snow peas and spring onions and stir-fry for a further 2–3 minutes, until all the vegetables are cooked but still crisp.

3 Sprinkle over the lemon juice and sesame seeds, toss to mix and stir-fry for a few seconds to heat through. Season with salt and pepper and serve.

Cumin-Glazed **CARROTS**

serves 4

PREPARATION 5 mins
COOKING 35 mins

16 whole baby carrots

1 teaspoon ground cumin

1 teaspoon ground cinnamon

2 tablespoons maple syrup

juice of ½ small orange

sea salt and pepper

¼ cup coarsely chopped fresh
   parsley

1 Preheat oven to 375°F/190°C.

2 Place all ingredients except parsley
in an ovenproof dish, toss to combine.

3 Bake until carrots are tender,
approximately 35 minutes.

4 Serve warm, garnished with parsley.

Desserts

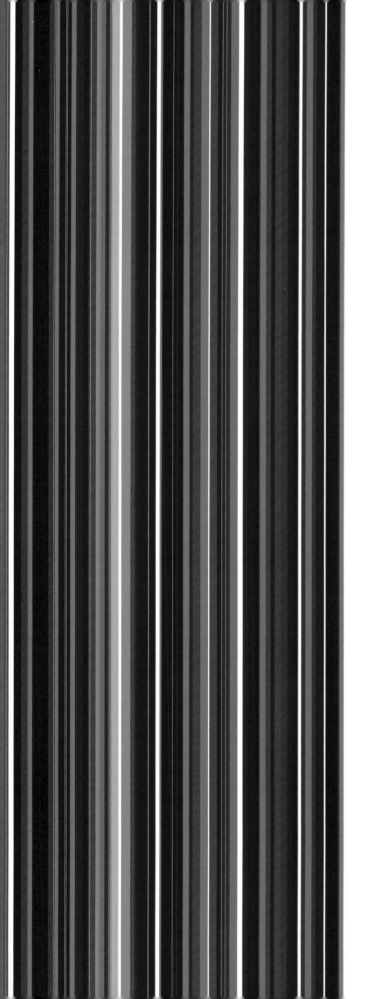

DESSERTS

BANANAS FOSTER *Smoothie*

serves *4*

PREPARATION	10 mins
COOKING	10 mins

TOPPING

½ oz/15g non-hydrogenated margarine substitute, such as Earth Balance

1 tablespoon raw sugar

2 tablespoons fresh orange juice

1 teaspoon ground cinnamon

1 large banana, thickly sliced

SMOOTHIE

1 large banana, broken into thirds and frozen until firm

1 cup vanilla low-fat yogurt

½ cup low-fat milk or soymilk

2 tablespoons wholewheat graham cracker crumbs

½ teaspoon vanilla extract

½ cup crushed ice

1 Melt the margarine substitute in a small skillet over medium-low heat. Add sugar and stir well.

2 Add orange juice and cinnamon. Heat until mixture gently bubbles. Add banana slices and cook for a few minutes until banana pieces are just warmed.

3 Allow to cool slightly while you prepare the smoothie.

4 Place all smoothie ingredients into blender and blend until smooth.

5 Pour into glasses, garnish with topping and serve.

Gingered PINEAPPLE

serves 4

PREPARATION **4 hrs**

1 pineapple

¼ cup dark rum

½ in/1cm piece fresh ginger, finely chopped

¼ cup shredded coconut

¼ cup honey

1 tablespoon chopped fresh mint

9 oz/250g strawberries

1 Cut pineapple in half, then in half again so it is in quarters. Remove hard core. Score pineapple with a sharp knife by cutting across and then lengthwise along the fruit. Do not cut through the skin of the pineapple. This will leave the cut fruit in the shell.

2 Mix the remaining ingredients well and spoon over the pineapple. Cover and refrigerate for 4 hours.

3 Eat within 24 hours. Trim and halve the strawberries and serve with the pineapple.

GUILT-FREE *cheesecake*

serves 4

PREPARATION	15 mins
COOKING	1 hr 10 mins

1½ cups wholewheat graham cracker crumbs

1½ oz/45g non-hydrogenated margarine substitute, such as Earth Balance

1 cup low-fat cottage cheese

2 cups plain non-fat yogurt

½ cup raw sugar

1 tablespoon wholewheat pastry flour

1 egg

2 egg whites

2 teaspoons pure vanilla extract

1 Preheat over to 350°F/180°C. Stir graham cracker crumbs and margarine substitute until combined. Press into an 8 in/20cm springform pan.

2 Bake for 8–10 minutes. Cool on a rack. Reduce oven temperature to 300°F/150°C.

3 In a blender or food processor, blend the cottage cheese and yogurt for at least one minute. Add sugar, flour, egg, egg whites and vanilla. Beat until smooth.

4 Pour filling into crust. Bake until top feels dry when lightly touched, approximately 60 minutes. Cool completely. Seal in an airtight container or bag and refrigerate for at least 8 hours.

5 Slice cheesecake and serve with fresh blueberries and raspberries.

DARK *Chocolate* FRUIT FONDUE

serves 4

PREPARATION 5 mins
COOKING 5 mins

6 oz/170g dark chocolate,
  broken into chunks

1 mango, peeled and
  cut into chunks

4 kiwis, peeled and
  cut into chunks

12 strawberries, halved

4 bananas, cut into large
  chunks, or seasonal fruit
  chunks of your choice

1 Put dark chocolate in a small saucepan
that has been placed over a large saucepan
filled with boiling water. The small saucepan
should just touch the water in the larger pan.
Alternatively, the chocolate can be melted
in a fondue pot over a flame.

2 Melt chocolate, stirring constantly.
Keep melted chocolate warm.

3 Place fruit pieces onto skewers, dip into
melted chocolate and enjoy.

CHOCOLATE *Pudding*

serves 4

PREPARATION 1 hr

COOKING 5 mins

⅓ cup cocoa powder

¼ cup cornstarch

1 cup raw sugar

2 cups low-fat milk or soymilk

½ oz/15g non-hydrogenated margarine substitute, such as Earth Balance

1 cup fresh fruit, for example, blueberries, chopped strawberries or raspberries

1 Put all dry ingredients into a saucepan with the cold milk. Stir and place on the stove. Bring to a boil, stirring constantly, then simmer for 2 minutes.

2 Add margarine substitute and stir. Pour into serving bowl. To prevent a skin from forming on the pudding, place a sheet of baking paper directly on the pudding surface while still warm.

3 Cool, decorate with fresh fruit and serve.

STRAWBERRY *Shortcake*

makes 12

PREPARATION	15 mins
COOKING	15 mins

2 cups wholewheat pastry flour

¼ teaspoon salt

4 teaspoons baking powder

2 oz/60g non-hydrogenated margarine substitute, such as Earth Balance

2 egg whites

1 cup low-fat milk or soymilk

1 tablespoon honey

1 cup chopped strawberries

1 Preheat oven to 400°F/200°C.

2 Place flour, salt, baking powder and margarine substitute in a bowl. Blend with pastry blender or rub with fingers until the consistency of coarse breadcrumbs.

3 Add egg whites and milk to make a soft mixture. Add iced water one teaspoon at a time, if needed to keep mixture soft.

4 Roll out on a floured board. Cut with a scone cutter or drinking glass about 2 in/5cm in diameter. The shortcakes should be about 2 in/5cm high.

5 Place on a baking sheet, allowing enough space between so they can rise. Bake for 15 minutes until lightly browned. Cool completely.

6 Drizzle the honey over the strawberries. Serve the shortcake with the strawberries and garnished with fresh mint.

BAKED *Apples*

PREPARATION 10 mins	
COOKING 40 mins	

4 large baking apples, cored

½ cup white wine or white grape juice

¼ cup honey

1 tablespoon ground cinnamon

¼ teaspoon allspice

1 teaspoon ground ginger

2 tablespoons raisins

½ oz/15g non-hydrogenated margarine substitute, such as Earth Balance, melted

1 Preheat oven to 375°F/190°C.

2 Place the cored apples in a baking dish, then pour in the wine or grape juice. Mix the remaining ingredients in a bowl, then place a quarter of the mixture in the center of each apple.

3 Place in the oven. Bake until tender, approximately 30–40 minutes. Baste apples with pan juices a few times while cooking. Serve warm.

APPLE *Blueberry* CRUMBLE

serves 4

PREPARATION	10 mins
COOKING	45 mins

½ cup raw sugar

4 oz/120g non-hydrogenated margarine substitute, such as Earth Balance

4 oz/120g wholewheat flour

4 oz/120g flaxseed meal

pinch of sea salt

¼ teaspoon baking powder

2 cups blueberries

2 cups coarsely chopped apples

¼ cup honey

1 Lightly oil an 8 x 8 in/20 x 20cm baking dish. Preheat oven to 375°F/190°C.

2 Cream sugar and margarine substitute. Work in flour, flaxseed meal, salt and baking powder. Mix with fingers or pastry blender until mixture resembles fine breadcrumbs.

3 Place blueberries and apples into the baking dish. Drizzle with honey. Pour crumble mixture over the fruit.

4 Bake for 30–45 minutes until topping is golden brown. Serve warm with a dollop of fresh plain yogurt sweetened with honey.

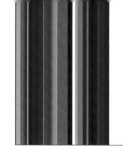

PLUM *Crumble*

serves 4

PREPARATION **15 mins**

COOKING **50 mins**

4 oz/120g wholewheat
   pastry flour

1 teaspoon cinnamon

1 teaspoon mixed spice

2 oz/60g non-hydrogenated
   margarine substitute, such
   as Earth Balance

2 oz/60g raw sugar,
   finely ground

1 lb/500g plums, halved
   and stoned

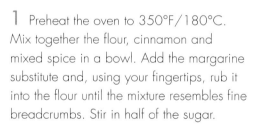 Preheat the oven to 350°F/180°C. Mix together the flour, cinnamon and mixed spice in a bowl. Add the margarine substitute and, using your fingertips, rub it into the flour until the mixture resembles fine breadcrumbs. Stir in half of the sugar.

2 In another bowl, mix together the remaining sugar and the plums. If the fruit tastes particulary sour, add a little more sugar to taste. Arrange the fruit in a 9 x 6 in/23 x 15cm ovenproof dish and spoon the crumble mixture evenly over the top.

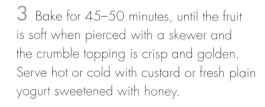 Bake for 45–50 minutes, until the fruit is soft when pierced with a skewer and the crumble topping is crisp and golden. Serve hot or cold with custard or fresh plain yogurt sweetened with honey.

Crumbles are a wonderful way of using summer or autumn fruits when the fruit is plentiful and cheap. Plum crumble is especially good, but you can use apples, rhubarb, blackberries or even peaches.

FRUIT *Ices* AND CHOCOLATE *Ices*

serves 4

PREPARATION 5 mins

BERRY ICES

1 cup strawberries

1 cup raspberries

1 cup blueberries

¼ cup fruit juice

2 tablespoons honey

1 tablespoon raw sesame seeds

CHOCOLATE ICES

3 bananas

¾ cup soymilk

3 tablespoons cocoa powder

2 tablespoons honey

1 teaspoon ground cinnamon

¼ teaspoon vanilla extract

¼ cup almonds

FRUIT ICES

1 Place all ingredients in a blender or food processor and blend until smooth.

2 Adjust sweetness by adding a little more honey if desired. Pour into popsicle molds, insert sticks and freeze overnight.

CHOCOLATE ICES

1 Place all ingredients in a blender and blend thoroughly until very smooth.

2 Pour into popsicle molds, insert sticks and freeze overnight.

You don't have to use just these ingredients – you can make these popsicles with your favorite seasonal fruit.

INDEX

Apple Blueberry Crumble	170
Arugula Salad with Citrus and Pomegranate	76
Asian Green Bean Stir-Fry	148
Asian-Style Salmon Fillets	100
Baked Apples	169
Baked French Fries	150
Baked Monkfish with Hazelnut Crumb Topping	104
Bananas Foster Smoothie	162
Beet and Bulgur Salad	80
Bircher Muesli	23
Buckwheat Pancakes	27
Bulgur Salad with Grilled Peppers	79
Butternut Pancakes	28
Caribbean Gazpacho with Avocado Salsa	40
Char-Grilled Tuna with Peach Salsa	94
Cherry Tomato Salad	68
Chicken Breast with Olives and Red Peppers	91
Chicken Breasts with Fruit Salsa	84
Chicken Pitas with Eggplant Purée	88
Chicken Stir-Fry with Lemon and Mango	90
Chocolate Ices	172
Chocolate Pudding	167
Classic Herb Omelette	30
Cod in Parchment	106
Cod with Macadamia Nuts and Mango Basil Sauce	92
Cumin-Glazed Carrots	158
Cumin-Spiced Carrot Soup	38
Curried Cream of Vegetable Soup	56
Curried Lentil Soup	48
Dark Chocolate Fruit Fondue	166
Dee Dee's French Pumpkin Soup	58
Dhal with Ginger and Cilantro	132
Easy Vegetable Stir-Fry	126
Fettuccine with Grilled Vegetables	120
Fish Baked in Corn Husks	112
Fish Stew with Lemongrass and Coconut Milk	109
Fragrant Cauliflower	152

Fragrant Salmon Stir-Fry	101	Lemon-Roasted Vegetables	144
Fresh Fruit Salad	22	Marinated Mushrooms on a Bed of Leaves	66
Fresh Fruit Smoothie	25	Melon Papaya Salad	62
Fruit Ices	172	Minestrone Piemonte	54
Garbanzo, Roasted Tomato and Garlic Soup	51	Mixed Bean Soup	55
Gingered Pineapple	164	Mixed Seafood with Spicy Sauce	114
Greek Salad	71	Mixed Vegetables in Tomato Sauce	140
Green Bean and Feta Salad	78	Muesli/Granola Parfait	26
Green Vegetable Stir-Fry with Sesame Seeds	124	Mushroom and Goat's Cheese Strudel	130
Grilled Brie with Beet Salad	67	Mushroom Feta Parcels	136
Grilled Salmon Steaks with Mint Vinaigrette	102	Oven-Baked Cod with Lime and Fresh Herbs	105
Grilled Tenderloins with Spiced Pumpkin	86	Papaya Fruit Salad	20
Guilt-Free Cheesecake	165	Peanut Soba Noodles	128
Harvest Vegetable Bake	146	Plum Crumble	171
Herb Rice Salad	72	Poached Salmon with Asparagus	97
Indian-Style Spinach	147	Pomegranate Exotica	64
Japanese Noodle Soup with Fresh Tuna	36	Porcini Mushroom Soup	49
Layered Fruit and Yogurt with Bran	24	Red Onion, Zucchini and Tomato Pizza	133

Roasted Tomato, Red Pepper and Bread Soup	44
Roasted Vegetable and Broccoli Couscous	122
Roasted Vegetable Salad	65
Roasted Vegetables with Mozzarella	154
Salmon with Asparagus, Balsamic and Orange	98
Simply Seasoned Cod Fillets	108
Smashed Potatoes	151
Snapper with Wine and Parsley	113
Snow Peas and Carrots with Sesame Seeds	157
Soy-Glazed Fish	110
Spiced Fish, Tomato and Garbanzo Soup	37
Spicy Wild Rice Salad	74
Spinach and Almond Soup	39
Spinach with Sesame Seeds	156
Strawberry Shortcake	168
Stuffed Chicken Breast	87
Stuffed Tomatoes with Garbanzo Beans and Cilantro	137
Summer Shrimp Pasta	116
Sweet Potato and Tofu Curry	127
Sweet Potato, Couscous and Leek Soup	47
Thai Spiked Pumpkin Soup	46
Thick Minestrone with Pesto	52
Tofu Stir-Fry	123
Tomato Ginger Soup	34
Tomato Salad	70
Tomato, Lentil and Basil Soup	50
Tuna Steaks with Tomato Salsa	96
Tuna with Roasted Plum Tomatoes	95
Tuscan Bean and Bread Soup	57
Tuscan Vegetable Terrine	138
Warm Spinach Salad with Walnuts	75
Watercress Soup	43
Wholewheat Burrito	134
Wholewheat Waffles	29
Yellow Pepper Soup with Red Pepper Harissa	42
Zucchini, Bean and Tomato Medley	155